PENGUIN MODERN CLASSICS

Pleasure of Thinking

Wang Xiaobo was born in 1952. From 1968 to 1970, he worked on a farm in Yunnan, China, as an 'educated' youth. He published *Golden Age* in 1992, first in Taiwan, but publication in China soon followed, where it was an immediate success, still topping bestseller lists today. Wang Xiaobo died of a heart attack in 1997, at the age of forty-four.

WANG XIAOBO

Pleasure of Thinking

Translated by Yan Yan

PENGUIN BOOKS

PENGUIN CLASSICS

UK | USA | Canada | Ireland | Australia
India | New Zealand | South Africa

Penguin Books is part of the Penguin Random House group of companies whose addresses can be found at global.penguinrandomhouse.com

First published in the United States of America by Astra House 2023
First published in Penguin Classics 2023
This edition published 2024
001

Copyright © 2023 by Wang Xiaobo, published by special arrangement with Astra Publishing House
Translation © 2023 by Yan Yan
'The Silent Majority' English translation copyright © 2008 by
Eric Abrahamsen

The moral rights of the author and translator have been asserted

Printed and bound in Great Britain by Clays Ltd, Elcograf S.p.A.

The authorized representative in the EEA is Penguin Random House Ireland, Morrison Chambers, 32 Nassau Street, Dublin D02 YH68

A CIP catalogue record for this book is available from the British Library

ISBN: 978–0–241–63326–7

www.greenpenguin.co.uk

Penguin Random House is committed to a sustainable future for our business, our readers and our planet. This book is made from Forest Stewardship Council® certified paper.

CONTENTS

My Spiritual Garden | 1

The Pleasure of Thinking | 5

The Maverick Pig | 19

War in the Belly | 25

Thinking and Feeling Ashamed | 31

Letter to a New Year (1996) | 37

Concerning "The Greatness Tribe" | 41

Interrogating Sociology | 45

What Kind of a Feminist Am I? | 53

On the Question of Homosexuality | 59

Li Yinhe's *Sexuality and Marriage in China* | 65

Li Yinhe's *Procreation and Chinese Village Culture* | 69

Overcoming the Puerile Condition | 75

The Feeling of Domestic Product and Cultural Relativism | 85

Letter to a New Year (1997) | 89

Odd Jobs | 95

Tales from Abroad: Clothes | 101

Tales from Abroad: Food | 105

Tales from Abroad: Housing | 109

Tales from Abroad: Travel | 113

Tales from Abroad: Thieves | 117

Tales from Abroad: Farm | 125

Tales from Abroad: Chinese Restaurants | 131

Why China Doesn't Make Sci-Fi Films | 143

Movies, Chives, Old Newspapers | 147

Beginning with the Internet | 153

Visiting the Home of an American Leftist | 157

My Approach to Reeducating the Youth | 161

Why I Write | 165

Using *Golden Age* to Talk About the Art of Fiction | 173

On Writing Style | 177

On the Literature of Repression | 181

Culture Wars | 185

Italo Calvino and the Next Millennium | 191

The Silent Majority | 195

PLEASURE OF THINKING

MY SPIRITUAL GARDEN

WHEN I WAS THIRTEEN, I often stole books from my father's cabinet to read. At the time, political tensions were high so he locked up all the books that weren't fit to be seen. There were Ovid's *Metamorphosis*, Zhu Shenghao's translation of Shakespeare's plays, and even a copy of *The Decameron*. The cabinet was locked, but my older brother had a way of prodding it open. He also had a way of convincing me to steal: you're small, your body is fragile, I don't think father will have the heart to beat you. But in reality, on the issue of beating me, my father clearly wasn't the gentleman he looked. My hands and feet weren't yet nimble, so he always took the opportunity. Anyway, we both read the stolen books, but the beatings were mine alone. That was how we read. Even though I got the short end of the stick, I bear no regret.

After reading *Metamorphosis*, I became fascinated with ancient Greece. My big brother told me: in ancient Greece, there was a type of philosopher who walked around wearing loose robes. One day, a philosopher went to see a friend. When he saw that the friend wasn't home, he asked for a wooden board on which to draw using wax. He drew a line on the board, gave it to the friend's family, and went home. When the friend returned and saw the board, he was impressed by the elegance of the line. He immediately went to hide outside the philosopher's home and waited until the philosopher left. He then asked for a wooden board and carefully drew a line on it . . . of course, the rest of the story isn't hard to imagine: the philosopher returned home, saw the wooden board his friend left, and got another board on which he drew another line, a line imbued with his heart and soul. He offered the board to his friend once more, thereby earning his utter and complete respect. In retrospect, I think my older brother made up this story. Back then, I thought about it for a long time before finally chuckling: how wonderful. Thinking back on it after thirty years, I'm not the least bit embarrassed. Even a frog at the bottom of a well has its own piece of heaven. A thirteen-year-old child can certainly have a spiritual garden. Besides, it's nice to have an older brother. Which isn't to say that I have anything against our nation's one-child policy.

Only as an adult did I begin to understand what a career in arts and sciences would mean. My brother went on to become a disciple of the late great logician, Mr. Shen Youding. I went on to study sciences. We shared an understanding of true and false as well as our experiences of thermodynamics, but those are stories from my twenties. When I got older, I traveled overseas. In Cambridge, I saw the apple tree where Newton felt the all-encompassing force of gravity; and Byron's Pool, which Lord Byron limped his way into for a swim. But always, I think back to that childhood moment when I gazed up at the stars of human wisdom. Every skyscraper has a foundation stone; the first passion remains irreplaceable. Perhaps every sage and poet has once felt that moment, as a child, of being awed by the stars. I've always felt that for a person, such passion, like sex, is indispensable.

I often go back to my childhood and think about problems through a child's heart. It makes many conundrums easier to ponder. A person's life should be spent accomplishing something, and it should be some sort of a cultural achievement; say you had to walk down a road, if there was some pedantic old scholar pointing and whipping your way across, then you wouldn't really be finding your way—you would just be reciting cultural genealogy. I've heard that that was how the Soviets educated their youth: they had to memorize a whole volume of Pushkin, half a volume of Lermontov, and remember that Russia was the homeland of the elephant (Shostakovich said a lot in his memoir). As for how we educate our youth here, I won't bother to elaborate, so as not to offend my colleagues. I highly doubt that knowing your cultural genealogy is the same as having a spiritual garden, but I'm not here to convince anyone. Hans Christian Andersen wrote "The Thorny Road of Honor" in which he explains that a life in the humanities is like walking through a field of burning thistles, and that sages and humanists alike walk in that fire. Of course, he was referring to all of the worldly trials and tribulations people have gone through in history, but to me this is not worth overthinking.

Through a pair of quiet, childlike eyes, the road looks more like this: a path between two rows of bamboo fences; the fences are blooming with purple morning glories, and on each stamen is a blue dragonfly. Such a description reeks of romanticism but if you wanted to convince Andersen of the simplicity of it all, this would be the sort of language you would have to use. Wittgenstein said before his death: tell them, I've had a wonderful life. The impression this sentence gives is: he had walked on that path of morning glories. Though I haven't gotten a clue about Wittgenstein's accomplishments, I still feel like we're two peas in a pod.

I have trouble grasping the following insight: to regrow the spiritual garden, recover the spirit of humanity, it is necessary to eliminate amateurs—the first to be eliminated should be the most popular amateurs. If by this, they mean that the money in readers' pockets is limited, so by buying other people's books, readers no longer have the money to buy my book; therefore, I need to eliminate them, then I can understand; but this insight doesn't seem very sophisticated. Even if it were, I wouldn't agree with it—we should be more like businessmen, adhering to the principles of the market and resisting uncompetitive practices. To turn my ideas into the new reigning paradigm is not something I want, or dare to want. As such, I should explain the motivation behind my essays (including this one). To be frank, I don't have a clear explanation. I can only say: suppose I died today, I wouldn't be able to say like Wittgenstein: I've lived a wonderful life; nor could I echo Stendhal and say: I lived, I loved, and I wrote. I am deeply afraid of ending up with nothing at all to say, which is why I am still hard at work.

THE PLEASURE OF THINKING

1

Twenty-five years ago, when I was stationed at a commune in the countryside, I brought a few books with me, one of which was Ovid's *Metamorphosis*. The people in our production team turned its pages again and again, read it over and over, until it was practically a roll of seaweed. Then, people from other production teams borrowed it, and I saw it show up in a number of other places. Each time, its shape further deteriorated. I believe that eventually, the book was read until its pages disintegrated. Even now, I can't get the image of its pathetic state out of my mind. Working in a commune meant hardship. There wasn't enough to eat. Difficulty in acclimating to a new environment led to illnesses. But the worst part was that there were no books to read. Had there been more books around, *Metamorphosis* wouldn't have met its tragic end, and we wouldn't have had to forgo the pleasure of thinking. I don't think I was alone in this experience: sitting under the eave after dusk, watching the sky fade, feeling alone and forlorn, recognizing we were being deprived of our own lives. At the time I was still a young man, but I was already afraid that my life would go on that way, that I would grow old like that. To me, that would have been worse than death.

At the commune where I was stationed, army representatives ran our lives. Nowadays, I believe they were all good and simple people, but I also believe that in my life, no one has ever made me suffer more than they did. For them, the pleasure of thinking entailed twenty-four hours a day of Maoist thought, which meant briefings in the mornings, reports in the evening, and, for leisure, seeing musicals about how "*yagpo du*"[1] they were. I had nothing against the songs and dances in particular, but after seeing the same show twenty times, they made me weary. Had we been caught with our books, it would have been a disaster. Even a book "by Lu Xun" would not have been safe—the only exception was the Little Red Book. By the way, this one person did in fact get in trouble by possessing an old copy of Lu Xun. One trick that may become useful again in the future is to take an interesting book and hide it within the covers of a boring book. I didn't think I could ever derive any pleasure from religious-like rites, so I was mostly always depressed. Stories like these have been written about by other writers as well. Take Stefan Zweig, for example. He wrote a novel about this theme entitled *Chess,* which is considered a modern classic. But I don't think he fully captured our kind of suffering.

---

1. *Yagpo du* is a Tibetan phrase meaning "good." It is the main theme of a popular propaganda song of the time.

The sort of suffering I'm talking about isn't like being locked up in a hotel with no books to read and no one to talk to, but lies in being free outside with the same sense of isolation, in the company of others who are suffering in the same way. Before us have lived countless great thinkers like Russell, Newton, Shakespeare, whose thoughts and works can free us from this suffering, but our access to their thoughts and writings had been severed. If a person wanted to find pleasure in thinking, their first wish should be for education. I admit, when faced with this sort of suffering, I lacked fortitude, but I was certainly not the worst of the lot. Take Mr. Bertrand Russell, for example. When he was five years old, he felt alone and isolated; he thought: if I lived to the age of seventy, then I would be only one-fortieth of the way through my misfortune! But when he got a bit older and was exposed to thinking—to the sparks of wisdom—his ideas changed. Had he been sent to a commune, he might have killed himself.

When speaking about the pleasure of thinking, I am reminded of my father's fate. My father was a philosophy professor. In the fifties and sixties, he worked on the history of thought. In his old age, he told me that his entire academic career was like one long horror film. Every time he tried to make a point, he had to look for a niche in the great architecture of official thought, like an old hen in the crowded courtyard of a big family looking for place to brood an egg. In the end, even though he loved his science and worked very hard, he was never able to find pleasure from a life of thinking, only horror. After a lifetime of research, he only left behind some ruins and vestiges that were anthologized in a book called *Logical Investigations*, published posthumously. As everyone knows, for a scholar of his generation to leave behind even only one book was not bad at all. This was precisely because in those years, there were people who wanted to make the Chinese mind completely insipid. In our country, there are only very few people who feel there is pleasure in thinking, but there are quite a few people who have felt the horror of even trying to think. This is why even now, many people believe that this is how thinking should taste.

2

After the Cultural Revolution, I read a piece of nonfiction by Mr. Xu Chi about Goldbach's conjecture. It was a rather romantic essay. When someone writes about things they don't really understand, it is easy to romanticize. In my opinion, for a scholar to be able to exchange ideas with peers is a basic pleasure. When Mr. Chen Jingrun[2] was sitting in a tiny room by himself proving mathematical theorems, he would have been in desperate need of foreign periodicals to read, and of the opportunity to converse with foreign colleagues, but he couldn't. So perhaps he could be considered unfortunate. Of course, he was probably more fortunate than people with no theorems to prove at all. To spend ten years proving a theorem, even if the moment of success feels like absolute bliss, doesn't add up to much average happiness. But to sit fruitlessly alone is so much worse. Had I known about mathematical theories when I was at the commune, I would have done as Mr. Chen did; even if I would not have been able to prove anything in the end, I wouldn't have had any regrets; a story like that would have been even more tragic than the story Mr. Xu had written. On the other hand, my highest sympathy isn't reserved for those who were deprived of the pleasures of learning, exchanging, and advancing ideas. I reserve my highest sympathies for those who have been deprived of *interestingness* altogether.

After the Cultural Revolution, I read a short story by Mr. Ah

---

2. Mr Chen Jingrun (1933–1966) was a Chinese mathematician who made significant contributions to analytic number theory. At the end of the Cultural Revolution, Mr. Xu Chi wrote a biography about him which became a national sensation.

Cheng about playing chess as an intellectual youth. It was also a very romantic story. Of all the chess games I've played in life, four-fifths of them took place during my time at *the* commune. There, I went from a not-too-bad chess player to a hopelessly mediocre hand. Whenever I think about the words "chess" and "commune" together, my body revolts. To play chess only because there was nothing else to do is tantamount to jerking off. I would never put something so boring into a story.

It is to the person who eats the same food everyday, does the same work every day, watches the same eight model operas[3] so many times that they know the next half of every line, that I offer my highest sympathy. Here I echo a line by Bertrand Russell, "To know the long and short, thick and thin, is the basis of happiness." Indeed, most of what is diverse is created by subtle thinkers. Of course, some will disagree. To them, uniformity is the basis of happiness. Lao-tzu wanted everyone to "empty their mind and fill their bellies." I don't like the sound of that at all; Confucians of the Han dynasty eliminated the Hundred Schools and ordained Confucianism as the sole discipline. To me that was a vile thing to do. Sir Thomas More imagined utopia in the finest detail but, like Mr. Russell, I would not want to live under such circumstances. At the end of the line are those good and simple army representatives. They wanted to wipe everything out of my mind except for that 270-page *Little Red Book*. In some domains of life, a certain degree of monotony and mechanical repetition is unavoidable, but thinking should not be included in such domains. A wandering mind isn't necessarily exceptional, but what is exceptional is logical

---

3. During China's Cultural Revolution (1966–1976), Jiang Qing, the wife of Chairman Mao Zedong, produced revolutionary model operas. They were the only officially permitted literary form at the time and told stories of revolutionary struggles and ideals. Many were made into movies. The operas were considered revolutionary and modern, in contrast to the traditional Peking operas, which were mostly regarded as "bourgeois" and therefore banned.

and novel thinking. The greatest misfortune in this world that we live in is that some people categorically reject novelty.

I think the happiest period of my life was when I first started college because to me science was a novelty. Its logic was complete and flawless, something rare in this mundane world. At the same time, it revealed the intellectual might of our forebears. It felt like a contest against a brilliant chess player—though outmatched at every turn, at least I was able to marvel at their moves. Among my classmates and people my age, many had the same experience. Despite repetitive actions like eating, defecating, and fornicating also offering some pleasures, these were much too simple to even compare to this other kind of pleasure. Art can also offer similar kinds of pleasure, but only at the hands of truly great masters at the level of Newton, Leibniz, or Einstein. For now, no Chinese artist rises quite to that level. But to be frank, the only works that can offer the pleasure of thinking are the ones that epitomize human wisdom. Anything less can only bring misery; and these mediocre creations tend to be motivated by utility.

3

The idea that there is a need to "indoctrinate" the organ of human thinking (the brain) is still very much alive today. I believe that the mind is the human organ crucial to perceiving supreme happiness, even more so than the organs of perception. Shoving "useful" thoughts into it seems suspicious at best. Some people say that the brain is a tool for competition, so one should learn to speak before birth and memorize Tang poetry before the age of three. But if this is the way you use it, how could you ever find joy? Truly troubling. Sure, knowledge can bring happiness, but if you distill it into a pill and swallow it, it no longer bears any pleasure. Of course, if anyone wants to treat their children like that, it is none of my business. I can only express sympathy for those children. Still others believe that the brain is a tool to make themselves look virtuous. To that end, they study a bunch of aphorisms and principles—in reality, they are only trying to make themselves seem better than they are. Truly pretentious. It pains me just to think about it, and I condone it. The worse are those people who use all sorts of reasons to eviscerate the diversity of thoughts necessary for happiness. They mainly reason it has to be done in the name of morality, but the standards they use are dubious. They believe that if you could fill the brains with good thoughts, there would be peace under heaven. To this end, they are willing to treat young people the way the army representatives treated me back in the day. But if thinking is the most important facet of human life, then changing other people's thoughts under a utilitarian banner is basically like murdering them for their happiness. It just does not make sense.

Some people believe that a person should be filled with only high-minded thoughts and be relieved of all the lowly ones. Such an idea may sound good, but it fills me with terror because I am precisely an amalgam of high and low thoughts; if a part of that is removed, my identity becomes a question. I hold all the respect in the world for high-minded gentlemen, but if you had to pluck out my brain and replace it with theirs, I would refuse, unless you could somehow prove to me that I am evil to the extreme and deserve death. So long as a person is alive, the continuity of their thoughts ought to be guaranteed. Not to mention, the high and the low are all being measured from one's own perspective. If I accepted them unconditionally, it would be like letting well-thinking hens lay eggs in my brain. But I would never concede that the thing on my neck is actually a chicken nest. Back in the day, the army representatives saw me as a lowly person. They wanted to force their thoughts and lifestyle onto me, like a brain transplant. Henry Fielding once said that there are few, if any, people who are both good and great. Therefore, this sort of brain transplant would have given me not only goodness but also stupidity. I hate to say it in such a utilitarian way, but in the real world, stupid people can't accomplish anything. Of course I hope to become a better person, but only my betterment is the result of having become smarter, and not the other way around. Besides, Heraclitus explained long ago that good and evil are one. Just like uphill and downhill are the same road. If you don't know what is evil, how can you know what is good? So the thing they really want is for people to have no thoughts of their own at all.

Suppose I believed in God (which I don't), and was troubled over the question of good and evil: I would beg God to make me smart enough to be able to distinguish between the two. I would never ask Him to make me stupid enough to allow others to inculcate me with their standards. If God asked me to take up the responsibility of inculcating others, I would beseech Him to make me choose between that task and Hell, and I would unhesitatingly choose the later.

4

Were I to cite the kindest moment in my life, I would cite the beginning of my time as an intellectual youth. Back then, I thought only about the liberation of mankind and not at all about myself. Still, I must admit that at that time I was truly stupid. Not only didn't I accomplish anything, but I contracted a disease, and after tossing my helmet and abandoning my armor, I fled back to the city. It is now my belief that stupidity is the worst sort of misery; diminishing the intellectual capacity of mankind is the worst sort of atrocity. To teach ignorance is the worst crime committed by otherwise good people. Therefore, we should never lower our guard against good people. Had I been duped by an evil scheming villain, I could come to terms with it; but to have been duped by kind, dimwitted people is intolerable.

Were I to cite the least kind moment in my life, I would cite the present. Perhaps this is because I received some education, or perhaps because I have grown older, but if you were to ask me to go liberate a group of people, I would first want to ask who these people are and why they need help; then I would ask whether helping them is within my abilities; finally, I would wonder whether it actually helps anyone for me to run off to Yunnan to dig holes. When I think about it this way, I definitely wouldn't want to join a commune. If the authorities forced me to go, I would still have to go, but all the holes we would dig into the verdant mountains and all the landslides we would cause wouldn't be my fault. Normally, people believe that kind but stupid people are innocent. If this stupidity were caused by nature, then I would agree. But people are able to cultivate their intelligence, so stupidity later in life is no longer innocent—besides, there's nothing more convenient than playing the fool. Of course, that isn't to say the army representatives back in the day were crooks pretending to be dumb—I still believe they were good people. My conclusion is: assuming good and evil are relative, these moral judgments must be made with a fully developed intellect and expansive knowledge. Yet, when you actually try to convince someone who thinks they can tell good from evil that they should first develop their intellect and expand their knowledge, they will always say that you are asking them to take the long road. Not only would they refuse, but they would harbor resentments. I wouldn't want to offend anyone over anything too trivial.

Of course, I now have my own standards of good and evil and I don't seem to behave any worse than anyone else. To me, stupidity, paranoia, and intellectual bankruptcy are the greatest evils. By this standard, whenever someone says I am good, that's when I am at my most evil; whenever someone says I am evil, that's when I am at my best. Of course, I wouldn't want to push this standard onto other people because I believe that smart, open-minded, knowledgeable, unique people are the most trustworthy. With regard to this concept, I believe after the period of "eliminate the Hundred Schools of Thought,[4] ordain Confucianism alone," our country has missed out on a lot of opportunities.

Our people have always been locking up knowledge and repressing thoughts to inculcate goodness. As a result, many thoughtful individuals missed their opportunities to learn, exchange, and advance ideas, and died before discovering the pleasure of thinking. The thought that my father was one such case leaves me with a heavy heart; and when I think about the fact that the number of such thoughtful individuals are as countless as the sand in the River Ganges, I slip toward despair. The source of all this tragedy are of course various real-world problems. Great figures tend to think that if everyone in the world were as good as they were—or more precisely, thought the way they thought: "think no evil" and "battle the wolf of selfishness," then the world could be saved. The people who propose these ideas thought no evil and weren't selfish to begin with, but of course they wouldn't know what evil thoughts and selfishness were. That's why they are basically saying: what I don't have, you shouldn't have either. Countless thinkers were smothered because of that. The countless thoughtful individuals, as numerous as the granules of sand in the River Ganges, amount to a massive resource. Trying to contain their thoughts is like trying to stuff the ocean into a bottle. Truthfully, I see it still happening, that is to say, the search for stupid solutions to the world's problems. On these grounds, I believe that since the Han dynasty, our country has been committing an ongoing intellectual massacre; and the fact that I can think this means that I am one of the few lucky survivors. Aside from expressing my sorrow for the current situation, I can't think of much else.

---

4. The Hundred Schools of Thought were philosophical currents and schools of thought that flourished between 600 and 221 BCE. The intellectual society of this era consisted of itinerant scholars, who often served as advisers to state rulers on methods of government, war, and diplomacy.

5

Even though I have reached my doubtless years,[5] there is still one thing that confuses me: how come there are so many people who hate new and interesting things? The ancients have a saying: had heaven not produced Confucius, the eons would have remained like night. But I believe just the opposite. Suppose that somewhere in history there was a great sage who suddenly discovered all novelties and things interesting, revealing the ultimate truth such that there would be nothing left to be discovered, then I would prefer to be born in a time before such a great sage existed. The reason is that if the ultimate truth has already been discovered, then the only thing left for humanity to do would be to judge everything based on this truth. Ever since the Han dynasty, this is how the Chinese people have lived. I am not at all interested in such a life.

I believe that, of all the intellectual activities a person can undertake, nothing is simpler than placing a value judgment. Even if you were a male bunny, you would already make value judgments—big gray wolf bad, female bunny good. But the bunny doesn't know his nine-by-nine multiplication table. This fact explains why people with no other real abilities so love the domain of values. To place a value judgment upon oneself at least requires some sacrifice; to judge others is simply too easy, too comfortable. To say something this crass leaves me feeling a bit ashamed, but I offer no apologies. It is because unsophisticated people have caused us far too much misery.

Of all the value judgments, the worst is the following: you think too much, too deeply, beyond what most people can understand, and that's wrong. When we are experiencing the pleasure of thinking,

---

5. Idiomatic expression meaning "middle aged."

we aren't hurting anyone; the sad thing is that intellectualism always causes some people to feel left out. Of course, the pleasure of a thought cannot be felt by everyone, but that is not our responsibility. I see no reason to eliminate these kinds of pleasures, unless you count cruel envy as one of the reasons—in this world there are people who enjoy nuance and people who enjoy purity; I've never come across someone who enjoyed nuance to envy or harm those who enjoyed purity, but I have seen plenty of the opposite. If I can be said to know a thing or two about the arts and sciences, it is because they flow from the mighty river of the pleasure of thinking. The river is there for the benefit of all people, and not as some would have it, flowing for a few alone. In the same way, the people who take pleasure in thinking weren't born for those few either.

For an intellectual, the desire to become a champion of thinking is more important than the desire to become a champion of morality. Certainly, people are free to not think and be stupid; on this point, I have no disagreement. But the problem lies in whether people should have the right to think and make themselves smarter. The people who appreciate the former freedom think that overly complicated thoughts will give people headaches. That seems reasonable enough. But if you take a farmer from deep in the mountains and asked him to work in a chemical factory in the city, he too will get a headache from all the complicated plumbing. That's not a reason to eliminate chemical engineering. Therefore, it is good if simple people can see what they cannot understand as something that does not concern them.

If I were to once again find that the world around me is filled with Cultural Revolution era army representatives and moralizers, I would be surprised, but I would no longer be afraid. This is because I have already lived to the age of forty-two. At university, I once met a professor who spreads mathematics like it was happiness itself. He has made learning math a joy. I have met people who have inspired my search for wisdom. I have also been fortunate enough to have read books that I wanted to read—it has been an eclectic selection from Bertrand Russell's *A History of Western Philosophy* to Victorian era underground novels. The latter selection was extremely profane, but in the end I got to read the naughty ones too. Of course, I am most grateful to those who wrote the best books—for example, George Bernard Shaw, Mark Twain, Italo Calvino, Marguerite Duras, and so on, but I hold no grudge against those who wrote bad books either. I myself have written a few books. Though they haven't yet become available to mainland readers, at least I've finally felt something of the joy of creation. These tiny pleasures make me feel like I have done something with my life, which makes me happier than my father ever was, and happier than the young people who are currently suffocating in an intellectual vacuum. As someone who has experienced both happiness and misery, I wish for the next generation to have more space to experience happiness, more space than what I was afforded. And of course, this call is aimed at those whose ambition it is to become teachers of morality, like the army representatives back in the day.

THE MAVERICK PIG

AT THE COMMUNE, I fed pigs and herded oxen. Had there not been anyone around to manage them, those two animals would have known exactly how to live. They would have wandered around eating and drinking as they pleased, and when spring came they would have looked for a little romance. Of course, in such a scenario, their standard of living would have been very low; it would have been totally unremarkable. Then, people came along who sought to give their lives a little more purpose: every ox and every pig was given a livelihood. For the majority of them, these livelihoods were quite tragic: the former's was to work and the latter's was to grow meat. I don't really consider this something worth complaining about because my life at the time wasn't much more interesting than that. Aside from the eight featured model operas, I didn't have any other entertainment. Then, there were the minority of pigs and oxen whose lives had a different purpose. Take pigs, for example—boars and sows had other things to do in addition to eating. But from what I could tell, they weren't particularly thrilled about the arrangement either. The boar's purpose was to breed. In other words, our policy allowed for them to be studs. But the weary boar often put on an air of propriety that was usually reserved for meat pigs (meat pigs are castrated), and refused to jump on the sow's back. The sow's purpose was to rear the young, but some of the sows ended up eating their own piglets. In short, human management has made pigs as miserable as can be. But they still accepted it: pigs are pigs after all.

Managing every aspect of life is something of a specialty among humans. Not only animals, but they also like to manage themselves. I know that in ancient Greece, there was Sparta where they managed themselves into absolute bores. The purpose was to turn the men into intrepid warriors and the women into reproductive machines. The former became like fighting cocks and the later became sows. These are very interesting species indeed, but my impression was that they didn't much like their lives. But so what if they didn't like it? Whether it be human or animal, it is very hard to change one's own fate.

The following is the story of a pig who was unlike the rest. When I started feeding it, it was around four or five years of age. Nominally, it was a meat pig. It was long and black and lean with a pair of bright shining eyes. The fellow was as agile as a mountain goat, easily leaping over the meter-tall pig fence; it could even jump onto the roof of the barn, a bit like a cat in that regard—which was why it was able to roam around all the time and hardly spend any time in the pigsty. All the intellectual youths who fed pigs treated it like a pet, and it was my pet too—because it only got along with intellectual youths, allowing only us to get within three meters of it; had it been anyone else, it would have run. It was a male, it should have been castrated. But if you tried, even if you hid the hog knife behind your back, it would have been able to smell it. It would have stared at you with its big eyes and grunted ferociously. I always fed the rice bran porridge to it first; only when it had eaten enough did I mix the rest with weeds to feed the other pigs. The other pigs would get jealous and become rowdy. The entire farm wailed and howled but the pig and I didn't care. When it had filled up its belly, it would jump on the roof or try to imitate different sounds. It knew how to make a car noise and a tractor noise, all very convincingly; sometimes when it vanished for days, I assumed it had gone to look for sows in the nearby villages. We had sows here too, locked up in the pigsty where excessive farrowing had left their bodies misshapen. They were also dirty and smelly. It wasn't interested in them; the village sows were better looking. It left behind all sorts of tales but my time feeding pigs was short so my knowledge of them is limited, which is why I won't bother relating them all here. In short, all the intellectual youths who fed it loved it. They loved its unapologetic attitude and the way it lived life to the fullest. The country folks weren't quite as romantic. They said, the pig was deviant. The leadership hated it, a point which I will come back to. My feeling for it was beyond love—I respected it, so much so that I ignored the fact that I was more than a dozen years older than it and called it "big brother pig." As was mentioned, this brother pig was able to imitate sounds. I assume it had tried to speak like a human, but wasn't able to learn—had it been successful, we would have poured our hearts out to each other. But it couldn't be blamed. The vocal ranges of pigs and humans simply differ too much.

  Later, brother pig learned to make a steam whistle sound, which led to some problems. Nearby was a sugar factory that blew its steam whistle once before noon when the workers changed shifts. Every day at ten in the morning, my pig brother would jump on the roof and imitate the steam whistle. When the people in the field heard it, they returned—this was an hour and a half before the sugar factory was supposed to blow its whistle. To be frank, this wasn't entirely brother pig's fault; after all, it wasn't a kettle and the sound it made differed from that of the steam whistle in important ways, but the folks insisted they couldn't tell the difference. The leadership convened a meeting where they labeled it a counterrevolutionary who was ruining spring planting; they needed to take authoritarian measures—that was basically the spirit of the meeting, but I wasn't worried for it—because if by *authoritarian*, they meant ropes and hog knives, then that would not even get them out the door. It wasn't as if the previous leadership had not tried, a hundred men couldn't catch it. Dogs were no use: brother pig ran like a torpedo, easily knocking a dog back a yard or more. But this time, they upped the ante. The political instructor led twenty some men, armed with all sorts of handguns; the vice instructor led over a dozen, armed with old-fashioned muskets, and they went out in two groups to hunt the pig in the clearing behind the farm. My heart was conflicted: considering the bond we had, I should have charged out with two hog knives and stood shoulder to shoulder with it to the end, but I realized that in doing so, I would have been upturning tradition—after all, it was only a pig; another reason was that I didn't have the courage to rebel against the leadership; I suspect that was more of where the problem was. Anyway, I watched from the sideline. Brother pig's serenity won my total admiration: it calmly hid in between both the handguns' and muskets' lines of fires; no matter how much people yelled and dogs barked, it never left that center line. This way, if the men with handguns fired, they would kill the men with muskets, and vice versa; if both sides fired at the same time, they would have all died. As for it, it was small enough that it would probably have been fine. Like that, it went around in circles until it found an opening and charged through; it ran with abandon. After that, I only saw it one more time among the sugarcane. It had grown tusks. It still recognized me, but it didn't let me get close anymore. Its reticence broke my heart, but I support its desire to keep a distance with those who bore sinister intentions toward it.

I am forty years old now. Other than this pig, I have yet to see anyone with such a total disregard for the life that was set out for them. On the contrary, I have seen many people who try to manage other people's lives and many people who are fine with letting their lives be managed. For that reason, I continue to reminisce on this pig who went its own way.

WAR IN THE BELLY

ONCE WHEN I WAS young, I got sick and had to stay in the hospital. At the time, there weren't any doctors in the hospital, only members of the worker and peasant army turned health workers—all the real doctors were sent to remote areas to be reeducated in the ways of the lower- and middle-peasant class. On the other hand, what else would you call someone wearing a white gown but "doctor"? During my first day at the hospital, a doctor came to look at my test results, then listened to me all over with a stethoscope, and finally asked: what's your disease? Of course he didn't understand the test results. But even without a test you could tell what I had: my whole body was the color of day-old tea: I had jaundice. I told him, by my own estimation, that I had hepatitis. This incident happened twenty years ago and at the time, we had never heard of hepatitis B, much less hepatitis C, D, and E. There was just the one infectious hepatitis. Apparently, hepatitis didn't exist in China until the three-year famine[6] when people started to eat Iraqi jujubes—they called it jujube but it was really a palm date. Even though I had never eaten a palm date, I still got the disease. The doctor asked me what to do. I said, why don't you just give me some vitamins—that's how my disease was cured. To be honest, staying at the hospital did nothing to help my condition, but I still thought it was better for me to stay there. At least that way I wouldn't infect anyone else in my troop.

At the hospital, there weren't any distractions so the only thing there was to do was to watch the doctors perform surgery on people. The knife was always aimed at the appendix—at least they knew enough to know to not mess with any more complicated procedures. I'm not kidding when I say I watched surgeries. At the time, there often wasn't electricity and what electrical supply there was, wasn't stable. The surgeries were performed in a room with four glass walls. The sunlight was best at two in the afternoon so that's when they did the surgery—all the patients at the hospital could watch and bet on how many hours it would take to find the appendix. Later when I told my friends at the medical university about this, they didn't believe me. They said, are you sure an appendectomy can take several hours? You can choose to believe me or not, but of the surgeries I saw, never once did they find the appendix in under an hour. The ones who performed the surgery complained, the human appendix is too hard to find—several of them were trained as horse and mule veterinarians, and had experienced performing surgery on army horses. Horse appendices are large and mule appendices aren't small either; they are all

---

6. The Great Chinese Famine was a period from 1959 to 1961, widely considered to be one of the deadliest famines in history. It was one of the greatest man-made disasters of the 20th century, resulting from policies associated with the Great Leap Forward (1958–1962).

larger than human appendices. Even when taking into consideration relative proportions, human appendices are small. When we were chatting during breaks, I said to them: if you're not familiar with human plumbing, then maybe you shouldn't perform surgery on humans. You know what they said? "The more unfamiliar we are, the more we have to do it—the battlefield is the best learning place!" young people today may not be familiar with the words but the second half of the sentence came from the *Quotations from Chairman Mao*. Human organs and warfare aren't the same thing, but no one bothered to point that out. There was one thing that I found even more disgusting: every time they performed a surgery, they had someone new try it. That way everyone could learn on the so-called battlefield, and the appendix could never be found. Where the knife landed and how big to make the cut were all a matter of personal preference. But there is at least one nice thing I can say about them: even though some of the cuts veered left, some veered right, and some even hit the mark, at least all the cuts landed on the belly. We should be thankful for that.

At the hospital, I met a guy who had appendicitis. The doctor urged him to undergo surgery. I told him not to do it under any circumstance—if there was no other option, he should request for me to do it. Even though I had never studied medicine, I once fixed an alarm clock and even one of our troops' hand-crank radios. Those two feats alone made me more qualified than any of the doctors at the hospital. Perhaps it was bad luck on his part, but after opening his belly, they spent three hours and still couldn't find his appendix. The doctor panicked and pulled out all his entrails to rummage through. When I was a kid, there was a breakfast spot near my house that sold fried livers and braised intestines. Every day, at the break of dawn, the chef would be outside washing pork intestines. That's what it reminded me of. The sky was starting to dim so more helping hands joined in the search. My man got tired of waiting so he pulled the white curtain aside and looked for his appendix himself. Finally, just before the sun set beyond the mountain, they found it and cut it off. The sky turned black. Had they been a bit slower, it would have been too dark to see and he would have had to spend the night with his guts hanging out. Before that, my favorite dish in the world had been pork intestines; after watching that surgery, I have never wanted to eat any again.

It's been almost thirty years. The reason why I am suddenly reminded of watching other people's surgeries at the hospital is because I am still shocked by how confused people were back then; they may as well have been insane. Who knows, maybe in thirty years, looking back at the people and things today, it will look like we are insane too. In that respect, it seems like every thirty years, our level of rationality takes a qualitative leap forward—but I suspect this theory won't hold up. If rationality can advance in leaps like that, that's basically like saying people before us weren't rational. Take the events of thirty years ago for example, the wielder of the surgical blade held a living man's guts in his dirty hands and rummaged through it. Even though he said he was learning on the battlefield, I still think he knew it was all buffoonery. Therefore, I come to this conclusion: of all the absurdities in human affairs, even though historical background plays a role, it is usually not the deciding factor. The deciding factor is this: the person making a farce of things is opportunistically monkeying around. That is to say, he knew what he did was absurd but he did it anyway because it was fun.

We can push the inference even further: no matter what society is like, people need to take responsibility for their own actions—but for the writer of the essay to layout his point so nakedly is a bit embarrassing, so I will stop. My story about my hospital stay isn't finished just yet: as I stayed at the hospital, my hepatitis wasn't getting any better; my face got yellower and yellower; my man who underwent surgery couldn't get his cut to heal so he also got skinnier and skinnier. We partnered up and returned to Beijing to seek treatment. I got better the moment I came back but my man ended up back in the hospital for another procedure. The doctor in Beijing said, even though the appendix was removed, his intestine wasn't stitched up properly. The end of it fused to the cut on his belly and formed a fistula. The contents of the intestine were leaking out so the cut could never heal. The doctor added that it was fortunate the contents leaked outward and not back into the stomach or else he would have died. But my man didn't feel so fortunate. He said: damn, no wonder I'm always hungry, everything was leaking. My man certainly was generous. Had that not been the case, he certainly wouldn't have offered his own innards for others to learn how to battle.

THINKING AND FEELING ASHAMED

AS A YOUNG MAN I was stationed at a commune in Yunnan. The place had still been considered part of the savage outskirts of China only a few decades prior. For that reason, in addition to verdant mountains and pristine waters, the local culture was also pure and humble. When I was there, in addition to working the land, the local people also had another exhausting task: to present themselves as sophisticated people. Back then, at the beginning of every meeting, one had to say some trendy phrases to come off as an intellectual. This was easy for us, but for the old country folks it was a challenge. For example, when our captain wanted to offer some words about the work going on in the fields—which for him as a seasoned ploughman should have been a piece of cake—he had to start with some sort of fashionable phrase, and that stumped him. Judging from his quivering lips, he seemed to be about to say, "Down with private interest and bourgeois revisionism," a simple phrase, not difficult to utter—that is, for those like us, it was mighty hard for him. His face turned red as he swallowed one word after the next. Sweat beads the size of peas rolled down his cheeks, but he still couldn't squeeze out the phrase. In the end, what came out was: fuck it, there's more than one way to run a farm! After hearing his brilliant rendition, we rose up in applause. I like simple people and I think he spoke just fine. But he had a higher standard in mind for himself because he wanted to sound sophisticated.

They say that in the olden times in Poland, when country women from a certain village met each other on the road, the first thing they said was always, "the Saint Mother Mary may be praised"; when someone from another village heard this, they scratched their head and said, "Yeah, she could be praised, so why don't you praise her?" Such an interpretation misses the point. The point wasn't to praise Mother Mary but to show one's sophistication. Back in the day, when we used to start every sentence with "the prime directive says," it was for the same reason. In *The Dream of the Red Chamber*,[7] when Lin Daiyu and Shi Xiangyun are in the garden playing literary domino, suddenly a verse praising the queen mother pops out. The author probably thought that since Lin was an educated elite, she should speak with sophistication. As for our captain, he was after the same affect but he wasn't as eloquent as sister Lin. For some reason, trendy phrases made him feel so ashamed that he couldn't get them out of his mouth for the life of him; whatever came out inevitably included a couple of

---

7. *The Story of Stone* counts among the four great classical novels of Chinese literature. Written by Cao Xueqin in the mid-eighteenth century, it is also called *The Dream of a Red Chamber*. Divided into five volumes, it charts the glory and decline of the illustrious Jia family and is known for its psychological scope and its observations of Chinese society at the time.

swear words. As a result, all the male intellectual youths fell in love with him. Before every meeting, we would wait in silent anticipation. The moment he spoke, we rose in applause, which only made his problem get worse.

Once, our troop was playing a basketball game against another troop, and he was our team leader—you wouldn't believe it if I told you, our captain knew how to play basketball. Even though he wasn't a great player, he was always able to make sure the other team sustained injuries. Sometimes there was blood on a chest, sometimes there were swollen gonads; he was an impressive center, our victory depended on his fierceness—the two teams lined up on the basketball court. The captain from the other team read from the *Quotations from Chairman Mao*. Then, it was his turn. He managed to speak without any swear words, which was disappointing to those of us who were eager to applaud. Who would have guessed that the captain ended up getting a whistle blown viciously at him by the referee. He was berated: the highest order is the highest order and revolutionary slogans are revolutionary slogans, you can't mix them up! He was then taken off the court where he sat to a side with a green face. As it turned out, what he said was: the prime directive says, long live Chairman Mao! The referee felt that the sentence was incorrect. The prime directive refers to the things Chairman Mao said. The venerable old man never said "long live" to himself. So his words were indeed incorrect. But I didn't think there was reason to correct simple people, your own sophistication should have been enough. After having gotten the whistle blown at him, our captain never dared to speak again, with or without swear words. He practically became a mute...

All the trendy phrases back then basically said the same thing, which was "be loyal and obey authority"—that's not a secret; back then, everyone lionized loyalty. Yet even though the words were the same, some people felt ashamed to say them while others didn't. That's where the subtlety lies. The ones who felt ashamed weren't necessarily less loyal or obedient. Take our captain for example, he was actually the most loyal, obedient player on the team. But his sense of loyalty and obedience came from a feeling deep in his heart. It was almost a rather feminine attitude. It wasn't just obedience and loyalty but love. That was why he wasn't willing to lay it all out in public in that corny way. Our captain's loyalty was evident in his willingness to work hard and plant good crops; but to ask him to stand in public and talk about it was putting him on the spot. A good analogy would be dating. Some men like to show love through their actions and not say "I love you" too loudly. Our captain was one of those. Other kinds of people didn't feel that way so they could say those things without feeling corny; but that by no means meant they were more loyal or obedient in their hearts—similarly, some studs will say "I love you" with their every breath, but you don't really know if their love is real.

As I mentioned, the place where I was stationed had a pure and humble culture. The locals felt it was embarrassing to display their simplicity in public; as a result, being sophisticated became synonymous with feeling ashamed. It wasn't only the captain who felt this way, just about everyone did. The following is an illustration from my personal experience: once I was at the farmer's market buying things. The thing I wanted to buy was a jackfruit from this old Dai lady.[8] One thing I need to clarify is that at the time, the locals all thought that all intellectual youths were rich. They upcharged us such that we paid two to three times what the locals paid for everything. That was why when we bought things, we waited until the vendor wasn't paying attention, then threw down the correct amount of money, grabbed the item, and ran. Some people call this way of buying things stealing, but I didn't think so—of course, I no longer buy things in this way. That day, I didn't

---

8. The Dai are an ethnic minority native to China's Yunnan province. Their language is related to the Thai and Laotian languages.

have enough money on me so the amount of money I threw down wasn't quite enough. The old Dai lady—or as the locals say, *mieba*—came chasing after me, yelling and screaming. She yelled: "No way! So sophisticated! Down with private ownership and bourgeois revisionism . . ." and in my moment of weakness, the said jackfruit—also called cow belly fruit—was stolen back. As you now know, when this *mieba* said those sophisticated phrases, what she meant was: you should be ashamed of yourself! Those words really hit home, even now when I think about it, I still feel embarrassed: just for a bite of a cow belly fruit, I was called a sophisticated thinker. Oh, the shame.

LETTER TO A NEW YEAR (1996)

WE READ AND WE wrote—1995 went by just like that. To talk about the passing year like this, I cannot help but feel sentimental, a deep breath celebrating life's tranquility. In the past, we did not enjoy such tranquility in our lives. When we were young, every year could have been written into a thick book; then, it became a small pamphlet; then, only a few thin pages of notes. Now, all there is to say is this one phrase: read, write. On the one hand, we've come a long way from that tumultuous age. On the other hand, we do enjoy this peaceful life. For us, living like this is enough.

At the beginning of the 1990s, our professor—a historian—prophesied the twenty-first century like this: the halo of idealism has faded, humanity no longer holds onto transcendent ideals, wishing to pluck the stars from the sky, but has instead turned its attention to real problems. When everything tends toward tranquility, humanity has entered its elegiac middle age. We're not historians and we don't look at the world in such sweeping terms, but nevertheless, his words touched us deeply. In the past, we also wanted to pluck the stars from the sky and now our lives indeed tend toward tranquility. Does that mean that we have also entered our elegiac middle age? If that is the case, it does seem worth lamenting. A French politician once said: if a person in their twenties is not radical, they won't amount to anything in life; but if they are still a radical in their thirties, then they also won't amount to anything. This is how we interpret his words: charging forth with a gung-ho attitude won't necessarily get you results; on the contrary, calm and collected contemplation just might solve problems.

Many young people will say: how can a dull life provide any happiness. On this, we would have to disagree. Mr. Bertrand Russell once said: true happiness comes from constructive work. People can derive a certain amount of pleasure from destruction, but this kind of pleasure cannot compare with the joy of creation. Only the joy of creation reaches into the infinite, destruction always has its limits. Self-aggrandizement and narcissism cannot bring happiness. On the contrary, they are the origins of unhappiness. We wish to distance ourselves from the crooked path, and derive happiness from constructive work. Only very few people are privy to the pleasure of constructive work, and we happened to have been afforded this opportunity for happiness—that is, we had the opportunity to become intellectuals.

In the blink of an eye, almost eight years have passed since we returned from overseas. We've felt no regret about our decision to return. This isn't to say that we are more patriotic than anyone else. The people who live in this country don't feel nearly as strongly about their nation as foreign scholars make it seem. If there was a patriotic essay contest, Chinese mainlanders wouldn't necessarily be the winners. A life is like an open book. We wished for this book's beginning and end to have thematic cohesion. We didn't want to change topics halfway through, such that our life's purposes would change. We wanted our life's purposes to become even clearer to us, even if this would mean a quotidian existence; that was the reason why we came back. It was our choice and not necessarily one that will suit others.

If it were someone else writing this essay, they might start with how things are moving full steam ahead, but instead we are talking about our innermost feelings. You might think that this is too humble a perspective, but it isn't necessarily so. Even if the situation wasn't so great, we would still feel the same way about the country. So as things stand, we aren't in a rush to talk about the situation. Oh, by the way, our country really is making strides. Yet, from where we stand, if our society could show just a bit more rationality, and a bit more fairness and tolerance, that would be even better.

As the New Year's bell rings, we are a year older. It is a time for reflection and resolution. Regarding this past year, and all the other years we have been alive in this world, there should be some sort of a takeaway: even though life is full of disappointments, you can still choose between happiness and sorrow.

CONCERNING "THE GREATNESS TRIBE"

AN OLD CLASSMATE of mine returned from America to visit his family. We had not seen each other for almost eight years. He's not doing poorly: even though his salary isn't very high, he lives comfortably in a two-income household. Since last seeing him in America, he's moved on to his third home, upgraded to his fourth car, and as far as PC computers are concerned, the moment a newer, faster one comes out, he runs to buy it, so you can't keep track of how many of those have passed through his hands. He hasn't upgraded his wife yet, and isn't planning to, which is the part I like about him. Even though he hasn't ridden in a Rolls-Royce or stayed in a mansion on Palm Beach, and even though he doesn't hold a stack of stocks in his hands, only a buttload of debt, still, as we like to say in the Northeast, at least he has "spent" a good time. Right now, I am without a roof or a plot of land to my name, so of course, I am a little envious. But when we got together, this was not what we talked about—that would have been far too inane.

This brother and I have ventured in all four directions. We've farmed the land, herded livestock, worked in factories, and twenty years ago when we shared the same window in college, our hearts burned with the same fiery ambition, and together, we dreamed of accomplishing great things. By great things, I just mean making our dreams come true. As for what we dreamed about, I'm too embarrassed to mention now, so I'll just use other people's dreams as examples. Take the big boss of the Microsoft Corporation, Bill Gates—for example, when he was young, he wanted to take the unassuming little microprocessor of his day and turn it into a useful computer that everyone could own and use, ushering in a scientific era that would truly sweep across mankind—that's the stuff great dreams are made of. Today, this dream has largely come true, and he has made a significant contribution to that progress, truly admirable. But as for his business success, that seems less admirable to me. Another example would be Martin Luther King Jr. who once declared "I have a dream," and now on American campuses, you can see Black boys and girls strolling along with white boys and girls. From such a beautiful image, one can sense the greatness of Dr. King's dream. But fast-forward to the present, there's not much more for me to add, and my cheeks are starting to get hot. All I can say is that we once had these kinds of dreams too.

Every person has his or her own dream, but such dreams aren't always the start of something great. Mr. Lu Xun once wrote about a certain kind of person in his essay: his biggest dream was to cough up half a mouthful of blood on a snowy day and have his maid support him as he lazily ambled into the courtyard to enjoy the plum blossoms. When I read this, it made me furious: how can someone have a dream like that! At the time, I thought: if this old mister wasn't so particular about the snow, the plum blossoms, the maid, and just wanted to cough up some blood, then that's something I could help him with. At the time, I was a young man with muscles on my arms and a hard fist. Nowadays, I wouldn't offer this sort of help. I'm past that age. Now, when I look in the mirror and see a wrinkly face, I hardly recognize the person. When I'm walking on the street and come across a colossal object that upon closer inspection turns out to be the girl of my dreams from back in the day, I can't help but swallow a mouthful of cold air. When you swallow too much cold air, you start to forget things, so I should get all I have to say off my chest while I still can. Not every dream is the start of something great, but all great things start from a dream—of that I am certain.

Young people today have their "celebrity fan tribes" and "office worker tribes," but the ones who want to achieve greatness don't have a name so let's call them the "greatness tribe." Back in the day, campuses (whether it was in China or America) were full of these types. When Mr. Gates showed up on campus with his casual wear and a head full of messy hair, he was just like us, a part of the "greatness tribe." When I first got back to China, at least half of the students I taught belonged to the greatness tribe. Their eyes sparkled with the dream of greatness. I could always tell with one glance who was or wasn't a part of the tribe. But this tribe has gotten smaller and smaller, and one day, maybe they will go extinct like the dinosaurs. I asked this brother of mine, what are you doing these days. He said he sat around and helped people run software packages. I yelled at him in anger: people like us should be doing research—who wants to run software packages? But he said, they pay me, so who cares. It made sense. If someone paid me thirty or forty thousand American dollars a year to run software packages, I'd run his packages too. This shows that even I am no longer a part of the greatness tribe. But when we were young, we had grand dreams. The greatness tribe isn't a bunch of daydreamers, nor are they just loud voices in an angry mob; and they certainly aren't teenagers whose blood rises to a boil before they've even figured out what's going on. The greatness tribe believes that all beautiful dreams can come true—in other words, dreams that can't come true aren't beautiful to begin with. If you don't succeed, then you must have done something wrong; and if you succeed and the results aren't beautiful, but more like a nightmare, then you must have thought about it wrong to begin with. No matter how it turns out, this road must always exist—prepare a dream and prepare to work toward that dream. Whether or not this way of thinking is correct, I'm not yet certain. One thing I am sure about is: there exists a greatness tribe.

INTERROGATING SOCIOLOGY

LI YINHE RECENTLY FINISHED a study concerning women's emotions and sexuality. The report has been published in the *Chinese Journal of Social Sciences*, the monograph is being prepared for publication. This study did not use questionnaires or statistical methods, but instead adopted the interview methods of cultural anthropology—even though this isn't the study's only particularity, it is one worth mentioning.

From casual observation, Li Yinhe's methodology lacks mystique—after finding someone willing to be interviewed, first she figures out how to meet face to face: should she go to them, or will they come to her? After setting an appointment over the phone, they proceed to the next step.

If she goes to them, then she will grab her briefcase and hit the road. Inside the briefcase will be a notebook and a couple of ballpoint pens. She usually travels by public bus—because she is meeting someone new, she will have put on a little makeup, which for her is a deliberate gesture, though others may not notice it. In the capital city, the least fashionable, most casually dressed women are most likely the women professors and women PhDs. A woman PhD with makeup on is still a woman PhD, not a public relations lady ... like that, she has interviewed many people. It makes people feel that a professor or a doctor is just an ordinary person.

When the subjects come to her, they walk into her dormitory building and up a dusty stairwell. Her home is much like that of other intellectual types, filled with piles of books and papers. After pouring a cup of tea for her guest, she begins the interview. After the interview, if it happens to be time to eat, she will treat her guest to a casual meal. It is exactly the same as when a working-class person receives a friend. She has never offered to reimburse a guest's "taxi receipt," and her guests have never made such a request. They can probably tell from the way she looks that she isn't the taxi-receipt-reimbursing type. As her research progresses, more and more people have visited her home, but she doesn't see anything wrong with that. One day, an interviewee (this was a male friend, belonging to a different study) urged her: Professor Li, this is not good! You shouldn't invite so many strangers into your home. She thought about it, but didn't think it was a problem. Besides, there was nowhere else to meet.

Aside from this sort of anthropology with Chinese characteristics, there are other possible methodologies—for example, stratified sampling, surveys, and questionnaires. But these all require cooperation with some government body as well as the participation of a university sociology department. Suppose the subject of a study was a midsize city, you have to first randomly select a certain number of district offices, from which you then select a number of neighborhood committees. Only from there can you select individuals by their embroidered household registration booklets.[9] One important thing you mustn't forget is to make sure that the individual you choose adequately represents whatever profession or age group your study seeks to investigate. After the survey is finished, you then have to compare it to other statistical sets and census data to check if your study was in fact representative. Only by completing all those steps can your sampling process be considered scientific. That's how all the social science textbooks explain the process, except the foreign textbooks don't talk about district offices, neighborhood committees, or household registration booklets; instead, they mention phone books and church registries. Then there are the other things that neither Chinese nor foreign textbooks mention, which are how to find a large sum of research money and how to obtain the cooperation of the government. But seasoned sociologists can figure those things out on their own, so the research continues. A big group of surveyors (current class of college students), led by a group of neighborhood committee cadres, visit home after home. If the questionnaire involves sensitive topics, then the neighborhood committee cadre becomes indispensable. The fact is that some of those selected to be surveyed may refuse to answer. Under such circumstances, the overly enthusiastic young college student will begin to argue with the annoyed interviewee. Eventually, the latter asks the fatal question: what right do you have to ask me that? Why should I tell you? Unable to answer, the former will inevitably lose his decorum. That's the point at which the neighbourhood committee cadre can intervene and pull the latter aside and offer him or her some indoctrination and persuasion. Then, he or she will return and reluctantly answer the sensitive questions. Here I must emphasize that such a

---

9. Each household in China has a registration booklet called *hukou* that registers information about the family members. This includes information about household members' birth dates and places of birth, marriages, addresses, and number of children.

survey process isn't just some writer's fantasy. I have worked in these sociological research units. I know about these things. I always felt that when you come across interviewees who are unwilling to participate, the data they provide cannot really be considered scientific.

In my experience, surveys involve two great challenges, one being funding and government cooperation, two being the cooperation of the survey subjects. For most sociological research projects, the former poses a greater challenge; but when it comes to sensitive topics, the latter poses a greater challenge. To summarize: the first challenge is the obtainment of a representative sample. The second challenge lies in getting the interviewees to cooperate. When it comes to sexual topics, the second challenge is nearly insurmountable. A foreign example can help to illustrate this. Some years ago in America, they conducted a survey relating to sex. The first challenge was easily overcome. Congress gave out a huge grant to facilitate the research. The government even opened citizens' private information (their Social Security numbers) to the researchers, allowing them to select samples so excellent that it could make other sociologists jealous for a hundred years. But what happened after that left nothing to be envied. Among the people selected, many were unhappy to be included in such a study—they refused to answer. As previously mentioned, America doesn't have neighborhood committee cadres, and the police don't get involved in these things. So the researchers had to resort to another tactic: war of attrition. Once you were selected, even if you refused to answer, the researcher would come back again and again until you've answered. One person received fourteen visits, enough to annoy anyone to death. After that, the American sexologist could finally declare, with the confidence of a Gestapo officer: most of the people have answered. There were still a few stragglers, but even in the real Gestapo's interrogation chamber, there were a few tough nuts who died before they said anything, so the sexologist need not feel any shame. What was shameful was the results of their research: the data contradicted itself all over the place. For example, American men say that they have sex four to five times a month; yet American women say they have sex twice or three times a month. How can this difference be explained? In another example, the proportion of homosexuals among Catholics is much lower than among atheists. So the study shows that nonbelievers are more likely to be gay. I'm afraid even the pope himself wouldn't dare to stand behind that conclusion because there is only one reasonable explanation, which is that religion makes people afraid to tell the truth. In the end, even the researcher couldn't help but admit, some people didn't tell the truth. To be fair, compared to other types of sociologists, sexologists rarely have the opportunity to conduct large-scale studies. Having come upon such a once-in-a-lifetime oportunity, they were understandably overzealous and overlooked a basic fact, which is: if I want to tell you something, I will tell you; if I don't want to tell you something, even if you hang me up and beat me, I still won't tell you—besides, you don't have the guts to hang me up and beat me.

Of course, other than hanging someone up and beating them, there are other methods. For example, you can follow someone to a place with no one else around, knock them unconscious with a club and plant a listening device on their body. That way you can get reliable intelligence on their sexual activities within a certain time frame. Not only will the data be reliable, but you've also made use of cutting-edge technology, which will definitely satisfy those who like to stay ahead of the times. But this method isn't feasible either. If you were to accidentally hit someone too hard and kill them, this would be hard to explain. Sociologists are required to be law-abiding citizens as well; they can't just randomly hit people on the head. From this we can derive a conclusion: the subjects of the sociologist's study are people, not laboratory mice; you have to show them respect; all research must be done on the premise of the interviewee's willing cooperation. From this perspective, Li Yinhe's interview methods are praiseworthy. She mostly just invites people to tell their own stories—of course, she will ask questions of her own but only to fill in the blanks in what her counterpart has already talked about. If a question could make her subject uncomfortable, she definitely would not ask it. The reason is that questions that will make the subject embarrassed will make her feel embarrassed as well. I always feel that her results are reliable because she is operating within her own cultural context and with a day-to-day attitude. The results of this kind of research are much more valuable than fancy academic chicanery—the anthropologist Bronislaw Malinowski said as much in his forward to Fei Xiaotong's *Peasant Life in China*.

Imagine, back in the day, when Fei Xiaotong was doing his research in Jiang Village. It was a familiar place to him, practically his hometown; communication with the villagers was simple, he didn't need a translator; he could go anywhere he wanted to in the village without the accompaniment of the village chief. Like that, without even needing to try very hard, he collected his data and wrote his dissertation. His dissertation received the highest of praise from Malinowski. According to Malinowski, the report was invaluable precisely because it didn't require any sort of academic framework—years later, Chinese scholars have given this methodology its own academic name: grassroots sociology. I feel that Li Yinhe's methodology falls most closely under the purview of grassroots sociology. Yet in comparison, it might not even be considered sociology in the foreign sense of the term. Even though questionnaires and statistical methods are foreign inventions, the methods are in fact scientifically sound. When applying these methods, one must obtain government approval, so the result can be called official sociology. Some things just can't be helped; using the government's power to obtain the consent of the people isn't a good thing, any serious sociologist will have qualms. The conclusions

Chinese sociologists draw always seem to confirm the official view from above—perhaps it's all a coincidence, but official publications always somehow leave a bad taste in your mouth. When it comes to sensitive topics, official sociology runs into trouble. When faced with these problems, sociology must evolve. These new breeds of sociology need names. For example, the American sexologist's "war of attrition" method might be called interrogation sociology. And the example we used previously, where the subject was knocked unconscious and implanted with a listening device might be called forensic sociology. As we go down this path, sociology takes on more and more of a fascistic flavor; its methods smell more and more of Himmler's methods; its results smell more and more of Goebbels's. I don't like the smell of that at all. In contrast, Li Yinhe's methods, however modest, are at least free of these evils.

WHAT KIND OF A FEMINIST AM I?

BECAUSE MY WIFE WORKS in women's studies, I read a number of books on feminism and we often discuss our own perspectives on the matter. As intellectuals, it is hard to approach the topic of women's rights without some sort of an inclination. I feel that if a person doesn't respect women's rights, he or she can't really be considered an intellectual. But there are so many kinds of theories concerning women's rights (which I don't think is necessarily a good thing), that it really matters what kind you are talking about.

Socialist feminists believe that the inequality between the sexes is a result of social policies, and that getting rid of sexism requires the reform of social policies. In the West, this discourse takes on a coloring of class struggle, but in China that is not the case. As we all know, our country already practices socialist policies and promotes gender equality. Government actions promoting the social welfare of women have seen significant progress. But it is precisely under such circumstances that we find socialist feminist theories lacking. For example, as corporations are downsizing these days, many female workers have been forcibly laid off. If you pointed your finger at the corporate manager, he would retort: why don't you ask about these women worker's own abilities and work ethics? Stories like these have already received plenty of attention in the press. Clearly, a person's life cannot simply depend on social welfare alone, it also has to depend on personal effort. And the more social welfare one receives, the less personal effort one generally puts in. Just as other schools of feminism point out, when socialist feminists ask society for welfare, they are admitting to their own powerlessness, and that's not a small error. Under socialist policies, the people who receive the most welfare are generally the most envied—when I was young, everyone envied the workers at the state-owned enterprises because they received the best welfare. But welfare and dignity are two different things.

The pertinent question is: in our country, are men and women equal? On this, there is disagreement. The Chinese people believe that they have done well on this front. But some Western observers disagree. As for me, I think it is not one question but two. The first question is: in our society, are men and women seen as equals? There is difficulty in answering this question. As everyone knows, whenever there is the need, the authorities will set a gender quota at every level of government and every representative body. I even heard that in support of the 1995 World Conference on Women, publishers are putting out several collections by women authors. You can decide to read into this however you want; therefore, the whole thing loses objectivity and need not be discussed. The other question is: in our country, what actual statuses do women enjoy in terms of their abilities, accomplishments, and the powers they hold; are they comparable to those of men? This is a much more serious question and my opinion is: of course not. Women are entirely misrepresented—perhaps with the exception of athletic competition, but sports don't say much. Our country always approaches the question of women's rights from a socialist feminist framework, allocating to her all sorts of things including representation. In my view, this sort of attention isn't enough. Real accomplishments are earned, not allocated.

In the West there is the radical feminist perspective, which argues that women are superior to men. The fact that women are born peace-loving and environmentally conscientious is evidence of their superiority. Supposedly, women can have stronger and longer orgasms than men, which is more evidence of their superiority. I am highly suspicious of the seriousness of such evidence. Even though it is perfectly admirable for women to love their own gender, there is no reason to go overboard. Starting from the womb, men and women begin to differ, I think the difference is beautiful. Others might disagree but I think that having to determine what's better or worse just because there is a difference is a sort of market opportunism—being born a woman seems to me the better end of the deal. Of course, by this standard, China is full of opportunists who will do anything to have sons. To them, that's the better end of the deal. In the future, humanity will be left with only one gender—male or female. When those people learn that there used to be two genders, they will grieve and say: our ancestors sure were opportunists. Of course, around here, there are some women who wear the air of radical feminists. In Chinese, we say they have "tracheitis." It is my personal opinion that those with "acute bronchitis" aren't the best representatives of Chinese women. I tend to see the world through the lens of aesthetics rather than power dynamics, which makes me feel like an opportunist—but of course, that's something for others to judge.

Many Western feminists believe that sexuality is as essential to feminist theory as labor is to Marxist theory. Chinese people find this perplexing. Perhaps in some years, the Chinese will come to understand the reasoning behind such thinking. The current trend is to pigeonhole women more and more into the discourse about sex. As far as humans are concerned, of course sex is a very important topic. But to talk about it only in relation to women is unfair. Western women feel that in the sexual domain, they have lost a lot of dignity, which is reasonable. But if you go back to look at the Cultural Revolution, other than a few inches of hair, men and women felt no difference at all. Surely dignity was preserved, but at the cost of all the fun. Liberal feminists believe that men should offer pleasure to women, through which process women can preserve their dignity. If you don't agree with that, then you will have to choose between dignity and pleasure. As a man, I would rather make myself pretty in the hopes that it will help with a woman's dignity and never have to watch women turn into a colony of blue ants again.[10] Of course, for the radical feminists, my determination isn't nearly enough to reverse the darkness. Real determination would require me to undergo a sex change and castrate myself.

My wife is currently obsessed with postmodern feminism. This theory attempts to offer a whole new interpretation for the question of gender. I am in complete agreement that our interpretation of sexuality has been problematic—from the beginning of history, people have been troubled by sex and sexuality. At first, they tried to pretend and role play. Later, they tried to be eclectic and inclusive. Eventually, they ended up neither here nor there, going so far as to say anything goes—most of these mistakes were made by men—that much I can see, but it really doesn't have anything to do with postmodern feminism. These philosophers, the female disciples

---

10. A reference to the Cultural Revolution, when all citizens, regardless of gender, wore blue uniforms. As a result, there was not much perceivable difference between men and women.

of Foucault, have a far more complicated and erudite way of explaining it. I hope to learn something from them, but so far have not had any success.

As a man, I agree with liberal feminism, and I think that that's enough. Adopting such a perspective has given me a certain peace of mind, and I recommend that other men adopt it as well. I admit that men and women are very different, but this difference doesn't imply anything else. It doesn't imply that one gender is somehow superior to another gender and it doesn't imply that one gender is somehow more clever than the other gender. When a girl is born into this world, just like boys, she should have the right to pursue whatever it is that she wants. If what she ends up with is what she wanted, then that's perfect—if I were her father, I wouldn't wish for anything more.

ON THE QUESTION OF HOMOSEXUALITY

BEGINNING IN 1989, Li Yinhe and I started conducting research on homosexual men in China. After many twists and turns, we finally arrived at what we as researchers consider a satisfactory conclusion—the study was published and a book was written, titled *Their World*. From the perspective of sociology, the book has significant flaws as well as significant merits. Its chief merit is being the first to discover that there is in fact a widespread male homosexual population on the Chinese mainland. This population has its own culture—we say culture in the cultural anthropological sense, meaning that all members of a group have some shared information. More specifically, they share information about spaces in which homosexual activities take place, how to recognize one another, nicknames they use, and knowledge about the social norms within the group. We conducted detailed interviews and described their contents. This is a type of scientific research.

The book's main flaw is that it does not take a statistical approach to sampling. Therefore, the results cannot be used for quantitative inference. Our interview subjects were all especially courageous and outgoing. They represent only a portion of the homosexual community and the information about the rest of the community is told through them. As a result, the findings may include some biases.

Some people have a fixed homosexual tendency. Whether or not they know what homosexuality is, or if they had experienced homosexual activities, such tendency still exists. Because of such a tendency, after experiencing homosexual activities, it is hard to turn the other way. On the other hand, there are those without the tendency who may have experimented with homosexual acts in their youth. But when they mature, they usually change and come to resent such activities. At present, it looks as if this tendency may be inherited, or in other words inborn. But it could also be a habit developed during childhood—we have discovered that first sexual experiences play an important role. One interesting thing is that everywhere in the world, no matter what ethnicity, culture, or religion, a certain proportion of people have such a tendency. When we talk about homosexuality, we are talking about these people. Current research suggests that permanent, lifelong male homosexuals comprise 1 percent to 10 percent of the male population. Our research confirms this point. Just looking at the size of the homosexual population we discovered, they definitely constitute more than 1 percent of the male population. But just how many there are, it is hard to know for sure. Suppose you had a child who is left-handed—you could forbid him from using his left hand to write and hold chopsticks, but his left hand will still be the nimbler hand. It is the same way with homosexuality. A person with homosexual tendencies may not have ever experienced any homosexual acts but he will still long for such a life. Our view is this: we should treat it like a natural phenomenon, even if its development may have something to do with one's childhood environment and culture.

Our investigation revealed that there are homosexual groups in all of China's major cities. They gather in public spaces to meet, to discuss, and when they find someone they are interested in, to form relationships. But the people found in these spaces comprise only a portion of the homosexual male population. More people tend to find love interests within their own social groups. In the latter case, the social activities involve more than just homosexuals. Some young people, no different from the ordinary, may accidentally befriend a homosexual. Given that the person is yet unmarried, it is hard to say if they willingly or unwillingly began to experiment in homosexual life. This shows that the difference between homosexuals and heterosexuals cannot simply be determined by their actions. The real line of demarcation lies in how a person chooses between a homosexual or heterosexual life. When we say that homosexual men comprise 1 percent to 10 percent of the overall male population, we are talking about lifelong, absolute homosexuals. Those who occasionally (once, twice, or for a certain period of time) engage in homosexual activity do not count. Besides that, we also researched and described homosexual life, the reason for choosing such a life, as well as values, world views, etcetera. The details are all written in the book and need not be repeated here. The main purpose here is to analyze the question concerning homosexuality and ethics, a topic that is not discussed in the book.

A person growing into adulthood is influenced by three main forces: the will of their parents, their circumstances, and their own volition. That a person becomes a homosexual is not due to the desire of their parents or their own volition, but rather circumstances. Even if it had something to do with genetic inheritance, a person's genetics can still be considered circumstantial. Since a person's volition isn't a factor, then their homosexuality is not a matter of morality or way of thinking. I think this is an important point. Homosexuals can exhibit negative behaviors like anyone else. They can, for example, be fickle, disloyal to their partner, dishonest to their wife and family, and so on; these can be considered matters of morality and ways of thinking. In these specific matters, a person should bear moral responsibility. But these are individual responsibilities and not the responsibilities of homosexuals as a group.

Most parents, including homosexual ones, will worry about their children being homosexuals because in our present society, homosexuals face a harsher reality than most people. Such a sentiment is understandable, however preventing a child from becoming a homosexual is not possible.

Not long ago, at a conference, there was a proposal to label homosexuality as a form of "social depravity," a category or phenomena that should be eliminated. Aside from shock, we also felt that these people certainly had very "high" hopes for society. Suppose society was a farm, these comrades would be wishing for all the crops to be neat and orderly, without a single weed, and every seedling must be perfectly identical. For those who think that homosexuals are a "sign of depravity," that must be their idea of "splendor." Unfortunately, human existence is a natural phenomenon. To call natural phenomena "depraved," is not a serious attitude. To put it simply, the point is this: some things are just the way they are, they cannot be manipulated by humans.

Today, we all know that what the Nazis did to Jews was an atrocity. But fewer know that they did the same to homosexuals. This is because homosexuals are not considered morally innocent. Their injuries did not elicit as much compassion and so they became weak and marginalized. Many of our interview subjects have been blackmailed and assaulted, but they did not dare to seek redress. There is a saying describing underhanded attacks that goes: beat the deaf, scold the mute, dig up the graves of one without progeny—now we can add another phrase: blackmail homosexuals. It's underhanded to beat the deaf because they can't hear what you're beating them over, so they don't know if they should fight back; scolding the mute is underhanded because they can't yell back; digging up the graves of those without progeny is underhanded because they have no descendants to come after you; blackmailing homosexuals is underhanded because they don't dare to report it to the authorities. These four types of abuses are equally malicious. In my view, these are the true forms of "depravity," and should be eliminated. Whether a phenomenon is depraved should be determined by the nature of the actions, and not by the identity of the group toward which those actions are directed.

Many fellow sociologists overseas are undertaking this type of work—to understand marginalized groups such as sex workers, homosexuals, ethnic minorities, and the entirety of the female sex relative to men. They want to improve their situations and change the detrimental ways in which people act toward themselves and others. They want to improve lives. Although our primary goal in researching homosexuals is to understand the truth, at the same time, we hope that our study can help the public understand the issues and acquire a modern, scientific attitude toward such issues.

LI YINHE'S *SEXUALITY AND MARRIAGE IN CHINA*

DR. LI YINHE'S NEW BOOK *Sexuality and Marriage in China* was published today by the Henan People's Publishing House and will be available to readers shortly. The book analyzes issues of sex and marriage in contemporary China using sociological methods. In addition to investigation and analysis, it references research from other countries, resulting in a comparative study. Based on empirical research, the results are reliable and discuss a topic of interest to the whole of society. With fluid prose and lively description, it is at once academic and highly readable.

Marriage, family, attitudes toward sex, etcetera, are important sociological subject matters as well as hot topics within society. In recent years, several works have appeared written by journalists and authors, with elegant prose and compelling narratives. In terms of raising public awareness of the subject matter, their contribution cannot be overstated. Their only shortcomings lie in a lack of methodological rigor and their over reliance on foreign and non-professional materials. Dr. Li Yinhe has received rigorous professional training and in writing this book, has conducted a series of studies. The publication of this book effectively addresses the shortcomings of sociological method and practice.

Social science is like natural science in that it requires an understanding of the subject matter above and beyond common sense. In other words, social sciences are also scientific specializations. Were this not the case, we wouldn't need experts. When experts discuss a topic, they should come to it with a unique perspective. This book delves into a wide variety of social phenomena. It tries hard to define an appropriate scope, pursue accuracy, and use a variety of methods of evaluation and analysis to reach a conclusion without placing necessary value judgement. The author's intent is to reveal reliable research to society, leaving critical judgment at the hands of the reader. Just as in other scientific disciplines, everyone simply wishes to report their findings objectively. Once the finding is released, it is no longer in the researcher's control. Whether or not it is valid will be decided by practice and the opinions of others. Experts only wish for others to know about their findings, and not to go out of their way to affect others or shock them. The validity of the finding should not depend on the reader's emotional response. The difference of approach will be clear once the reader has read Dr. Li's book.

In some of Dr. Li's research, she utilizes new statistical methods such as random sampling, LOG-LINEAR, LOGIT models, and such. Readers today have come a long way in their scientific training. Readers of sociology should naturally have a grasp of such knowledge. And readers from other disciplines will not be left entirely in the dark either. The author believes that probabilistic models are a common tool among many disciplines and can be understood by many people.

In some of her other research, she uses interviews as her method. A sociologist of an older generation from our country once said, sociological research should produce stories. A society comprises people with births, deaths, marriages and divorces, causes and effects, they can all form complete stories. For people of different cultures to understand one another requires an unbiased understanding of all the cultures. This is also what readers love to read.

There are also differences between the social sciences and the natural sciences. The subject of study of social sciences is human society, in which everyone lives. The subject matter of social sciences is not like that of natural sciences, in which only a limited number of experts have access. Everyone is a part of it, though. When people study people, there are easily biases. For example, egocentrism, cultural-centrism, etcetera.

The sociological profession in our country was passed down from one of the originators of modern social anthropology, Bronislaw Malinowski. Picture the venerable Mal back in the day inviting us to abandon the study and venture to every corner of the world, to leap out of the pen of mainstream culture. What a grand vision. Humanity is the total sum of everyone; most people does not mean all people. Meng-tzu once said: "Yang Zhu proposed individualism, that is to be without a lord; Mo-Tzu proposed universal devotion, that is to be without a father; without a lord or a father, one is but a beast."[11] To regard certain people as subhuman in this way seems rather unfair.

In Dr. Li Yinhe's book, a certain amount of attention is given to issues of sex and marriage outside of mainstream culture. For

---

11. Yang Zhu c. 440–360 BCE and Mo-Tzu c. 470–391 BCE were Chinese philosophers, the first advocating for self-preservation, the second believing that power should be based on meritocracy. Mo-Tzu was one of the first scholars to challenge Confucianism.

example, the voluntarily childless, homosexuals, the voluntarily single, and divorcees all have chapters devoted to them. The purpose is not to dwell on the exotic contingents in society, nor is it to affirm their views, but rather this devotion is the standard attitude of sociology and anthropology. In our country's traditional culture, there is a tendency to push one's views onto others. As a result, the Chinese appear to have only one kind of culture; everyone appears to adhere to one way of doing things. In reality all sorts of subcultures have always existed in China, only we usually choose not to see them.

I often cannot help but want to defend empirical research, perhaps it is unnecessary. In newspapers, I often see people criticizing the culture of childlessness, saying that it should not be encouraged. If some people say that Dr. Li is encouraging homosexuality just because she is discussing homosexual culture, that would be a bad thing. Sociologists study homosexuals for the simple reason that they exist. When we talk about different cultures, we are simply pointing to their existence. This study has nothing to do with encouragement. The empirical sciences study only what is there. It does not matter whether or not homosexuality should be encouraged. It only matters that it exists, that there are people being homosexuals out there. If only things that should be encouraged can be studied, then I'm afraid most of what we study will no longer be around, and most of what we see out there we'll know nothing about.

Of course, this book covers a much wider range of topics than just homosexuality. For example, mate selection, romantic love, marital finance, pubescent love, and more: topics that are relevant to a wider range of readers. The author's research brings attention to all sorts of attitudes toward the cultures of sex and marriage including their subcultures. It is hoped that other than the readers' own views of the matter, they will be able to understand the views and cultures of others as well. Such is precisely what modern sociology and anthropology hope to bring to society.

LI YINHE'S *PROCREATION AND CHINESE VILLAGE CULTURE*

RECENTLY, OXFORD UNIVERSITY PRESS published a new work by a female sociologist from the Chinese mainland titled *Procreation and Chinese Village Culture*.

Li Yinhe, in her study of the Chinese family and sexuality in rural China, brought up a new concept: the essence of traditional culture is derived from rural life. In China, a phenomenon ubiquitous from north to south is the presence of unplanned villages, large and small. This has to do with both agricultural practice and lifestyle. Furthermore, Chinese villages are densely populated, especially when compared with the villages of other countries. As a result, the cultural norm is this: in a village there isn't a wall that doesn't leak, everybody knows your business and you know everybody's business. This is the collective ownership of information.

According to the information school of anthropology, shared information is culture, therefore the existence of village cultures is unquestionable.

To my understanding, Li Yinhe initially wanted to use the term "commune culture" (*cun-she*/村社), but someone said "commune" already has a meaning and cannot be given a new definition. That is certainly correct, but I feel sorry for Li Yinhe's loss of the word *commune*. To be nuanced, the meaning of *cun* (村—"village") is clear and needs no explanation. The word *she* (社) is written with the radicals "deity" and "earth."[12] This is precisely the image she is seeking to invoke. In the village, the aunties and grannies are the deities of the earth, an omniscient network. Hence, an unplanned village is practically an information superconductor, without secrecy to speak of. Death and betrothal, marriage and birth: everything is public information, which is why nobody in the countryside makes decisions by thinking purely as an individual. This cultural phenomenon is crucial to understanding rural China. There are some who say that foreign culture is a culture of sin, while Chinese culture is a culture of shame. There is a sense of poignancy in this observation, but it is only a sense. Sinfulness comes from God; if you believe in him, you will feel like a sinner before him. But if you don't feel like there are always countless eyes on you, where would your shame come from? Without the collective ownership of information, it would be hard to explain the culture of shame.

Other than procreation, there are many things in a village that a person cannot make his own decisions about—for example, wedding ceremonies. Such events are expensive and painful beyond words, but you still have to play by the rules. Perhaps you would like to use concepts such as custom or tradition to explain this phenomenon, but you can't explain why people insist on carrying

---

12. Chinese radicals are components of Chinese characters that serve as semantic or phonetic indicators. They can be considered the "root" of a word or syllable.

on such a painful tradition unless you believe that everyone is a masochist. In fact, that is not the case. Who wouldn't want to take it easy? Village culture is a coercive force, an individual's will is no match for it.

Li Yinhe believes that traditional paradigms, namely clan consciousness, still exist in the villages, but that this does not necessitate their existence inside of the minds of certain individuals. In fact, they exist inside of the semi-isolated enclosure called village culture. This is also an interesting topic for discussion. We all know that in Scotland, there is a semi-isolated Loch Ness where a dinosaur still lives. The fact that in Chinese villages, there remain certain cultural dinosaurs should come as no surprise. In any case, under the present reign of the Communist Party, Meng-tzu philosophy of clans no longer has legal authority. But what still has authority is the village. Work is to be done by certain rules, problems are to be solved by certain logic, whether or not individuals want to. This is neither a matter of being antiquated nor a matter of clan regulations, but because there is always a big crowd of people staring at you. I believe this explanation more accurately reflects reality. She provides such an illustration: how you make your money is your business but how you live your life is everybody's business. In such a context, it would be difficult to reinvent daily life indeed.

The research for Li Yinhe's *Procreation and Chinese Village Culture* was based in the provinces of Shanxi and Zhejiang. Her approach is very fitting, but sadly the empirical work was not as rigorous as one could hope for. Suppose instead of studying a hundred some odd families across a couple of villages, the study comprised thousands of families, the results would be even more convincing. Of course, such an ambition would be close to a pipe dream. Her anthropological method emphasizes primary sources and requires face-to-face conversations. Even using a translator would have invited ridicule. The great anthropologist Margaret Mead conducted research in Samoa for years, but because she was mostly listening to other people's secondhand accounts, she was duped. In this light, a hundred some odd solid interviews is already pretty good. Indeed, the stories she describes have always been right before our eyes, only we never notice them. In the city of Beijing, there aren't villages but back alleys, courtyard complexes, and other places with very little outside traffic. In these places, privacy is also limited and it is hard to say if your personal decisions are yours alone. Because these phenomena are so close to our own lives, when you read this book, you will not doubt the reality of village culture.

The great Bertrand Russell once said: don't overlook critical thinking just because you have empirical methods.[13] Indeed, to propose an interesting hypothesis requires the serious work of critical thinking. What a reasonable maxim. As far as I can tell, she has really put in this serious work. Suppose death and betrothal, marriage and birth are all personal decisions, then there must be a logic—to pursue personal happiness or well-being. In the villages, such a logic is not really in vogue. What's in vogue is to do things in such a way as to elicit everyone's approval, or better yet, envy. It's a different set of values. As such, would it be appropriate to say that other forms of happiness and well-being don't matter to them? After the studies in Shanxi, before starting the Zhejiang studies, Li Yinhe wrote an essay for the magazine *21st Century*, discussing this topic. I cannot go into details here for the sake of space, but in short, the conclusion is this: no matter what, what one thinks is good and what other people say is good are still inevitably different, not one and the same. The reason why villagers put so much weight onto the latter is because they don't have a choice. The important thing is, it would be wrong to think that the

---

13. Bertrand Russell, British philosopher, logician, essayist (1872–1970), author of over 70 books including *The Problems of Philosophy*.

former doesn't matter to them. Once you understand this fact, the nature of village culture will be much easier to grasp.

Li Yinhe views village culture as a negative force because such a culture forces everyone to fixate only on the natural village before them. They put all of their precious resources into death and betrothal, marriage, and birth. The purpose of life becomes a never-ending pursuit of envy and glamour at the cost of improving one's life conditions. In such a culture, interpersonal relationships become domineering, squeezing out any sense of individuality. Others may disagree with her perspective—focusing on interpersonal relationships is precisely their strength. On this question, I'm afraid I will have to side with Li Yinhe because the Chinese village culture seems to go hand in hand with poor living standards. Moving into the city is the dream of tens of millions of farmers—therefore, village culture is just one of those things in whose participation one has no say in, regardless of whether one likes it or not. In this context, we cannot really sing praise to such a culture.

Li Yinhe is humble in her work. As a scholar, she is not the bombastic, loquacious type, nor is she the esoteric, pedantic type. What she seeks is clarity and common sense, even if such common sense will be seen by some as superficiality. On the surface, it seems like an academic has many objectives, for example, how many citations one receives, how many papers one publishes, how many monographs one writes, but for her these are not supremely important. What is most important is to discover something interesting.

OVERCOMING THE PUERILE CONDITION

N LI YINHE'S TRANSLATION of John Gagnon's *Human Sexualities,* chapter 17, "Erotic Environment,"[14] describes the evolution of America's attitude toward the censorship of works containing sexual content. For this reason, it is perhaps the most interesting chapter in the whole book. In the period just before the Second World War, America's censorship of "obscenity" was the strictest it had and has ever been. The works affected by these censorship laws extended far beyond what would be considered erotic works. As far as authors are concerned, not only were Hemingway's and Erich Maria Remarque's works banned, but even the

---

14. John J. Gagnon (1931–2016) was a pioneering American sociologist in human sexuality, whose work Wang's wife, Li Yinhe, translated into Chinese.

moral thinker Leo Tolstoy's works were listed. In the second decade of this century, America's banned books included not only Joyce's *Ulysses* and D. H. Lawrence's *Women in Love*, but even *Arabian Nights*, and Remarque's *All Quiet on the Western Front* could only be published in an abridged form. As luck would have it, I happen to have a Chinese edition of *All Quiet on the Western Front*. Not only is it abridged, but the cuts disrupt any sense of continuity. For me, the similarities are more than intriguing. In the past, when we talked about China's hypersensitivity to books and movies, we always attributed it to the different circumstances and social policies between China and the rest of the world. However, after comparing present-day China to America in the thirties one quickly acquires a new perspective.

After the First World War, America steadily ratcheted up its censorship of erotic works. While works of a sexual nature were heavily repressed on the one hand, on the other, the amount of sexual content in serious literature surged. As a result, from the federal to the state and municipal governments emerged frighteningly long lists of banned books. The victims included far more than the abovementioned authors. Even the Bible and Shakespearean plays had to be abridged before reaching the eyes of young readers. The Bible was stripped of the "Song of Songs." Shakespearean works were stripped of their supposedly obscene content. The result was that young readers could not make sense of anything. Of course, it wasn't just books that were censored; movies also could not escape the gates of censorship. Movies were prohibited from showing scenes depicting prostitution, sex, nudity, drugs, mixed-race characters (!!), sexually transmitted disease, births, and anything offensive to the Christian clergy.

The strict censorship of the time was based on certain theories. One theory supposed that any open discussion about sex (which isn't critical) would lead to a proliferation of sexual activity, because sexual education is the prerequisite for sexual behavior. In other words, human sexual appetite is so strong that even the slightest provocation will force it to manifest itself. Another similar theory went like this: sex is danger, people are weak, therefore, sex must be controlled to protect people. These perspectives bear much similarity to the present attitudes toward stricter controls. In our country, there are presently people who believe that adolescent sexual misconduct has to do with books and videotapes. Some parents suggest that after reading books relating to sex, their children's grades suffered. As a result, they propose restrictions on the sexual content allowed in books and video recordings.

In my view, because these opinions were put forward by people lacking scientific training, there are inevitable points of confusion. To take the American theories from the '20s as examples, we can only say that they are scientific hypotheses. They need to be tested before they can become theories, but the worst thing is that these hypotheses are so vaguely formulated that there is no way to test them. I saw a report in a magazine with statistics showing how many adolescents charged with sexual misconducted watched "indecent" books or pornographic videos. But this is the wrong way to arrive at a theory. The correct way to form a theory would be to point out how many of the adolescents who read "indecent" books committed acts of sexual misconduct. If we consider the rules of probability theory, these are two entirely different probabilities. There is no fixed relationship between them and they are not mutually substitutable. As for the parents to suggest that reading books with sexual content affected their children's grades, they are in fact proposing a model of cause and effect by proposing that reading certain books will affect their children's studies. Any experienced social scientist will agree that it is difficult to determine causality. To take the parents' complaint as an example, if you want to establish causality, you must show that the kids' grades went down *because* of the books they read; you must then show that there is no cause that led to both the children's consumption of such books and their declining grades. I personally know of a factor that causes both of those effects: the child's sexual maturation. Therefore, the abovementioned parents' complaint is unfounded. Kids nowadays are well nourished and enter sexual maturity early. Their demand for information about sex comes about earlier for them than it did for their parents' generation. As far as I can tell, this is the main cause for much of the public's concern about puerile sexuality. If parents only fed their kids steamed buns and pickled mustard, that would solve the problem (by delaying the onset of sexual maturity). The above analysis shows that, regarding the question whether erotic works of art have a corruptive influence on the young, popular common sense and expert opinion arrive at two very different conclusions. Were this not the case, experts would not be considered experts.

Of course, people accuse erotic works of more than just corrupting the youth, but also corrupting society at large. On this matter, the book provides a case study, which is the Danish experiment of the '60s. In 1967, Denmark permitted erotic fiction (genuine erotica). In 1969, they permitted erotic cinema, making it legal to produce and market pornography to citizens over the age of sixteen. The experiment produced two important findings: one, Danes only bought pornography during the onset of legalization, and then they stopped or bought very little. As a result, several years after the lifting of the ban, most vendors of pornography have disappeared from Copenhagen's residential areas. At present, there are only two small neighborhoods that still traffic in the porn economy, and these small-scale economies rely primarily on tourists to survive. John Gagnon arrives at the following conclusion: "People have many interests, of which sex is only one, and pornographic products represent only a small facet of such interest. Scarcely anyone makes sex their primary interest in life, and the number of those who make pornographic products their primary interest are fewer still."

The second finding of the Danish experiment is that the opening up of the pornography industry had a powerful impact on criminal behaviors. The volume of pedophilia cases dropped by 80 percent. Exhibitionism decreased significantly as well. Violent crimes (rape, smut) also decreased while the rates of other crimes stayed the same. This case shows that the legalization of pornography decreases rather than increases criminal behavior. Gagnon cites the case study not to promote his own agenda, but only to share its results.

After the Second World War, America's wave of censorship began to ebb. *Human Sexualities* offers the following perspective: the decline of censorship resulted from America's evolution from a conservative, primarily rural, homogeneous Puritan population to a diverse one. The former represents an anti-immigrant, anti-Black, anti-communist, xenophobic society under the control of the so-called moral police; when America became an urbanized, industrialized society, the conditions for strict censorship no longer existed. Such an explanation has deep implications for China. Our country is also predominantly rural. As for a Puritan tradition, we don't have that history. Puritans believe that human nature is evil and needs to be controlled. Our traditional philosophy believes that humans are by nature good, but that this intrinsic goodness disappears once we grow past the "age of innocence." Therefore, regarding their post-pubescent populations, the two cultures see eye to eye. *Human Sexualities* presents a timeline of the liberalization of America's attitude toward sex. I will list it here for reference:

Before the '40s: any nude female body part, or anything suggesting such, including raised skirts and outlines of nipples are prohibited;
1940s: backs of nude women appear in erotic magazines;
1950s: profile view of breasts;
1960s: breasts appear, vaginas appear in *Playboy* magazine

1970s: male reproductive organs appear in *Viva* and *Playgirl* magazines, female labia appear in *Penthouse* and *Playboy* magazines.

Every time a magazine went too far, the censors cried foul and warned that disaster would ensue. But in the end, there was no disaster. As a result, these people eventually met the fate of the boy who cried wolf.

Human Sexualities views the censorship of video and publishing as an example of a culturally specific sexual environment. Censorship's main target is erotic content, but serious works of art containing sexual content can also be also dragged under its punishing influence. By serious works, I mean works that relate to sex without treating sex as a primary subject. These include works of great literature and film, works of sociology and anthropology, and even medical and psychological studies. On some level, serious authors and filmmakers can also be considered experts. Try thinking about censorship from their point of view. What conclusions would they draw?

In the early days of Reform and Opening-Up,[15] Mrs. Nieh Hualing Engle and her husband Mr. Paul Engle[16] visited China and met with a group of our nation's older authors. At their meeting, Engle asked: "In your Chinese works, why isn't sex mentioned?" One elder author replied: "We in China aren't interested in that!" This was clearly pulling the foreigner's leg, as reality was not so. But the foreigner didn't take the bait, he asked: "You in China have so many little kids, what's up with that?" The subtext to the

---

15. This refers to the Chinese economic reforms led by Deng Xiaoping after Mao's death in 1976. Labeled as "Socialism with Chinese characteristics" their aim was to revive the stagnant economy by moving away from collectivisation and open up to private and foreign investment.

16. Paul and Nieh Hualing Engle were both writers in their own right and after Paul Engle retired from directing the Iowa Writer's Workshop, they jointly created the Iowa International Writing Program, which runs to this day.

questions is that the Chinese didn't produce all those children by pinching their noses and holding back their disgust ... did we? Of course, we could reply: "Yup, it was just like eating bitter medicine!" But that would have been like admitting we were a bunch of phonies. The truth is that sex is an important part of the lives of Chinese people. Our attitude toward the enjoyment of sex is no different than that of our foreign counterparts. In this area, there is really no need for a charade. Because it is important, we should naturally talk about it. Serious literature cannot avoid it; sociology and anthropology need to study it; art films should depict it. This is for the sake of science and art. But society wants to suppress the discussion, so it really isn't a question of the sexual environment but the intellectual environment.

Human Sexualities describes how the process of banning books occurred in 1920s America: a plaintiff would find a passage from a book and read it to a judge. Then they he would say: would you want your kids reading *that?* Like that, Hemingway, Lawrence, and Joyce were banned. I don't know if there are any Hemingways in our country but if there are, getting published must be a headache for them. Could Hemingway write something that would satisfy the plaintiff? I think not.

I am an author myself. No author can control who accesses to their work after it is published. Suppose a serious author wrote about sex. Even if the point of their book isn't to arouse or stimulate, but to create verisimilitude, it can't be helped if a young boy finds and masturbates to his novel. It's like society wishes to dictate to the author: because these boys exist, you cannot publish literature. How unfair is that? But this isn't even the worst of it. Applying the same standard to sociologists and psychologists is even more unfair. It's as if society wants every serious writer or professional author to imagine their target reader as a sixteen-year-old boy—not even a boy with dreams and ambitions, but the kind of teenager who is fundamentally lost in life.

I am a reader myself. In my doubtless years now, I enjoy academic books and serious literature alike. But on the marketplace, there is only the seventy-two-story version of *The Decameron*, the abridged version of *The Plum in the Golden Vase*, Remarque that has been butchered into nonsense, and a bunch of books on the sociology and psychology of sex that are, frankly, complete gibberish. Recently, I bought a copy of Foucault's *The History of Sexuality*, but I can't make heads or tails of it. So now I'm looking for an English version. These politics work to my great detriment. I can say without any reservation that I am a high-level reader, but the censors treat me like a sixteen-year-old boy.

Our country's publishing industry, working according to official logic, must consider the needs of the low but not the high. A book's eligibility for publication does not depend on the existence of a readership with artistic discernment and its benefit to that group. Instead, publishing is dependent on the existence of a group without discernment and the harm a given book may cause this hypothetical reader. To me, censorship isn't a question of sexual environment but intellectual environment. Other intellectuals feel the same way. This is not a point that the book *Human Sexualities* considers. In the '20s and '30s, Americans with an intellect such as Hemingway, and others, all went to Europe. But then, Hitler showed up and kicked all the intellectuals back to America; thereby, fomenting a golden age of cultural and scientific achievements. Suppose Hitler didn't burn books and kill Jews in Europe, I dare say that compared to Europe, America would still be a backward wallow. I wouldn't go so far as to say that the scarcity of talent in our country is due only to censorship, but I can assure you, that if a Hitler showed up in America, there would be a lot more talented individuals in our nation.

If the books on the market that I want to read aren't suitable for ignorant hicks, then books suitable for developing youths aren't suitable for intellectuals either. This has nothing to do with ideology. If for example, a book like *The Diary of Lei Feng,*[17] which is good for teenagers, is translated into English, it might very well be suitable reading for the students at West Point Academy. But for bald-headed professors, it wouldn't be very useful. Books like *Luo Lan Xiao Yu*[18] or the novels of Qiong Yao[19] might be suitable for American high school girls (unfortunately, they already have many books of the sort), but for those intellectuals over forty with a PhD lecturing at universities in sociology departments, they wouldn't be appropriate. If you were to force them to read such books, they may gag. These types of people might read *Story of O*, even if they don't admit it when you ask them. Some might argue that since the children are our future, we should sacrifice for them. But the problem is that the price of such a sacrifice is to turn grown-ups back into kids. The result is that we are left without a future.

In Europe and America, adults and children occupy separate intellectual environments. Some books and movies cannot be seen by kids. The logic behind such a strategy is to acknowledge that adults can control themselves, and do not need courts and churches to decide who can and cannot know what. This is not simply because this material bears no harm to adults, nor is it simply because these works include knowledge that they need, but because it respects the dignity of adults. The trend in modern society is for everyone to become an intellectual. Obstructing their access to knowledge is to obstruct their development. As Sun Longji points out in *The Deep Structure of Chinese Culture,* the Chinese people

---

17. Lei Feng (1940–1962) was allegedly a soldier in the People's Liberation Army, portrayed as a model citizen whose example the population was encouraged to follow. His story encourages selflessness, modesty, and devotion to Mao and the Party.

18. *Luo Lan Xiao Yu* is an essay collection by Taiwanese author and broadcaster Luo Lan (1919–2015), who gained fame for narrating the life experiences of people from all walks of life.

19. Qiong Yao (1938–) is the pen name of Chen Che, a hugely popular Taiwanese writer and producer whose romance novels have been adapted into more than a hundred films and TV dramas.

are caught in an intellectual environment characterized by the puerile condition, what Freud refers to as the anal stage. Perhaps, for various reasons, especially historical ones, we cannot avoid having some childish ways. But what then? One way is to maintain the puerile condition, the other is to overcome it, and prepare to grow up. Those who choose the former should also believe in the fictitious slogan in George Orwell's *1984*—"ignorance is strength." Those who choose the latter should also believe in Bacon's maxim—"knowledge itself is power." Of course, this next step doesn't mean rushing toward tomorrow, but it also shouldn't mean that tomorrow will never arrive.

THE FEELING OF DOMESTIC PRODUCT AND CULTURAL RELATIVISM

IN *THE WATER MARGIN*, Song Jiang broke the law and was stabbed, then exiled to the River Lands under the charge of Dai Zong. Customarily, he should have offered Dai Zong some sort of a bribe, but he refused to do so. As a result, Dai Zong had to ask Song Jiang to bribe him. Song Jiang still refused and questioned: "You are in no possession of some shortcoming of mine, what right do you have to ask me for ransom?" Dai Zong was furious: "How dare you question my right! You are a prisoner in my charge; I can construe even your coughing as a crime! You, fellow, are a piece of line product in my hands!" Domestic products mean shabby products. Dai Zong compares Song Jiang to a cheap item and himself to the proprietor of said item. I was twenty years old when I first read this story. Ever since then, I have been unable to shake off the feeling of being a piece of domestic ware or product. It is a tragic feeling. In this Eastern society I inhabit, there is nothing that can soothe my woe—this feeling of sadness does not derive from the literal facts of my existence, but from the unfortunate reality of domestic product—with which I feel affinity—itself. The thing that tells you you are a piece of domestic product is this: no matter what people decide to do with you, and no matter how they evaluate you, they don't need to offer an explanation or ask for your consent. I once had such an experience: when I was seventeen, I was suddenly put on a train and shipped off to Yunnan. On my body was a label that read: HARROWER OF THE HINTERLAND. To this I offer no protest; I only have this burning feeling of being a piece of domestic product. In the Chinese cultural tradition, there is an explanation: "Under all of heaven, not all land belongs to the king; between the water's margins, not all land belongs to the duke. . . ." It's true that under all of heaven, not all the land belongs to the king; I'm not the king; between the the water's margins, not all land belongs to the duke; I'm still not the king. To me, it would have been more direct if they had just said that I was a piece of domestic product.

The ancient Egyptians thought that the Earth is round—as you know, that's the truth; the ancient Greeks, though, thought the Earth was a flat board resting on the back of a giant whale. The whale drifted in the sea and when the whale got a back itch, it would scratch it, and you would have an earthquake—that's not the truth. Bertrand Russell pointed out that this wasn't because the Egyptians were smart and the Greeks were dumb. The Egyptians lived in a wide-open terrain. A look around revealed a curved horizon. It wasn't hard for them to reach the right conclusion. The Greeks lived in a mountainous coastline with frequent earthquakes. It is no wonder they thought about seas and whales. Identical people will have different understandings of their relationship to the environment depending on whether they live in an open terrain or in the mountains. If a person is born a piece of domestic product, their understanding will inevitably be different from someone born a proprietor of goods. An example of the latter perspective would be America's Declaration of Independence. This was written two hundred years ago by a group of North American plantation owners. By our standards, the document is full of brazen violations. As for examples of the former, the Chinese classics are full of them, starting from Confucius. Compared to the Declaration of Independence, they are full of domestic jargon. I am unsatisfied with their discourse and plan to offer my criticism. But I need a platform to stand on: I have to prove that I'm not a piece of product—as such, it is not proper to criticize the proprietor of products.

In recent years, cultural fever shows no signs of diminution. Western theories surge into China wave after wave. Some of these theories with Western origins are the stuff of my nightmares—these include cultural relativism, functionalism, etc., that said, culture is a tool for living (Malinowski's functional theory), no culture is any worse than any other (cultural relativism), and other nightmares. In principle, these perspectives are correct, but everything depends on how to apply them. In the hands of a crook, any good idea can be spoiled. Take for example Song Jiang in the River Lands prison. He lives within a special kind of culture (let's call it Song dynasty prison culture). According to the rules of this culture, he is a product in the hands of Dai Zong, he should offer Dai Zong some perks. If he says to Dai Zong, all men are equal and I am a man, so why do you call me domestic product? There is something wrong with this culture. Dai Zong can then say: Song Jiang, according to the principle of cultural relativism, there's nothing wrong with any culture. Our culture is fine just the way it is, so you should simply accept being my domestic product. Song Jiang might reply: perhaps the culture is fine, but for you to ask me for perks is an act of blackmail, I can't oblige. Dai Zong can then say: culture is a tool for living. If in our culture, you have to offer me perks, then there must be some function being served. Therefore, you should just offer me something. If you don't, then I will have to act in accordance with our culture and beat you with a stick—don't worry, beating you has its function too. This example shows that cultural anthropology cannot stand up to Dai Zong's misuse and abuse. In truth, no science can stand up to misuse and abuse. But there are some scholars who study Western sciences precisely to distort them using traditional Eastern thought. Using cultural relativism, they can indeed squeeze out the logic that we are all domestic products.

As we know, in Africa there is a custom of female circumcision, leaving scars on the female body and mind. Some African women are ready to fight to resist this practice. Suppose there are people in Africa who despise Western theories, they could say: this is our culture, you can't touch it. They might even bring up cultural relativism and offer a bunch of nonsense. Cultural relativism enables anthropologists to look at other cultures respectfully. It's not there to prove that Song Jiang is a domestic product, nor is it there to support female circumcision in Africa. So long as a person lives under the influence of their own culture, they have the right to criticize that culture. I offer criticism to the culture which I inhabit because I live here, under the influence of this culture. Suppose I got a green card and lived overseas and you said I didn't have the right, I would have to concede. A person should be the master of his own fate, not someone else's domestic product. If you can't even understand that, then you may as well be a walking corpse, and walking corpses don't have the right to talk science.

LETTER TO A NEW YEAR (1997)

A**NOTHER NEW YEAR.** The years have passed quickly. In the blink of an eye, forty some years have passed; it really is hard to believe. With the arrival of a new year, I should offer some pleasantries, but all I can think about are all sorts of strange things. When I was little, maybe six or seven, I saw something interesting: at the time, the grown-ups were busy working on a thing called an "ultrasonic." Anyone slightly older than me probably remembers it better than I do: you'd take a long iron pipe and smash it until it slit open on its side, then attach a sharp razor to the slit. When you ran cold water through it, the water hit the blade, creating a vibration that caused ultrasonic waves. The ultrasonic wave could not only steam buns but also heat up cold water. If this ultrasonic thing really worked, we would have never run out of hot water—not only would there be enough hot water, it would have solved all our energy problems. At the time, they placed these devices all over the public baths. You had to be careful when you showered or else you could cut your butt. The water would turn red but not hot—nowadays we still use natural gas to heat our showers. Clearly, the ultrasonic devices didn't work. The strange thing is, there was no follow-up. People stopped talking about it. It's like something I dreamed up, which is what makes it feel so strange to me.

Another thing happened twenty years ago. At the time I was an intellectual youth having just returned from the countryside. At the break of dawn, I took a trolleybus home. When I got to the alleyway, there was a small hospital. In the misty dawn's light, I saw lots of people lining up outside the hospital. Each person carried a basket. Inside the basket was a spunky rooster. At the time, I thought the hospital had closed down and was turned into a poultry processing center, and that these people were there waiting in line to get their chickens butchered. But who could have guessed that they were there to have the hospital staff draw blood from the chicken, to be injected into their veins? Supposedly, after shooting up chicken blood, a person's energy increases a hundredfold; this transfusion is allegedly so powerful that it can make the aged become young again. The people in line told me that in all the animal kingdom, roosters had the most vitality, up and crowing before the break of dawn. That was why shooting up chicken blood had a magical effect—but I didn't understand what was so special about roosters crowing early in the morning when the owls had stayed up all night. Every morning, I was woken up by roosters crowing before five in the morning. Who knows if it was the roosters crowing or the people crowing—if shooting up chicken blood could make a person as vigorous as a rooster, maybe it could make them crow at five in the morning too; this would certainly save on alarm bells. Of course, this story has no follow-up either. All of sudden, people stopped shooting up chicken blood and no one even talked about it again. It was like another dream.

Suppose these weren't just dreams that I had. Then these things would definitely be worth mentioning at the turn of a new year. People were always trying to invent new tricks and to use them to solve big problems. Forging steel with a rocket stove, using iron pipes to make ultrasonic waves, trying to use these strange methods to solve problems that could only be solved with modern industry; not to mention injecting chicken blood into their veins, drinking buckets of cold water, waking up in the morning to shake their arms out on the sidewalk, trying new methods to address problems yet unsolved by modern medicine—since I mentioned arm shaking, I should elaborate a bit: for a while, it was said that shaking your arms could cure all disease. A a result, there were always people standing on the street shaking their arms like a bunch of wobbly toys. Maybe you've done some arm shaking too, but no longer remember it. All of a sudden, arm shaking was no longer allowed. It was said that an evil counterrevolutionary invented the exercise in order to deliver a poisonous message: that the Chinese people should shake off their beliefs and call communism quits.... The most recent trick is this: suppose you got cancer, don't go to the hospital, call for a qigong master. He can grasp at the air and pull the cancer right out. From the point of view of science, these tricks can only be described as strange. But the practices I've mentioned so far weren't even the strangest developments in Chinese culture. The strangest things that have happened to us belong to the domain of knowledge....

I don't know if people still remember that during the Cultural Revolution, there was a wave of workers, peasants, soldiers reading philosophy. They said philosophy was the study of wisdom. People who studied philosophy could become so smart that they could solve all problems. If you patiently studied philosophy, it probably would make you a bit smarter. But what people studied at the time wasn't really philosophy, but rather simple tricks and incantations. It was a bad idea to doubt these tricks: this would brand you as a backward element, or even a counterrevolutionary. Even though I was perfectly revolutionary, I never believed that the incantations held any wisdom. Either way, that was how these strange things were born. Even now, the intelligentsia continues to invent new tricks and incantations. Every time they discover one, they rush forth like the villain in the movie *Landmine Warfare*,[20] and declare: I know the secret about the land mine! Amid the excitement, we learned about "the third wave," "postmodernism," and learned to talk about everything through the lens of culture; if that was your angle, you were smart. As an intellectual, I have great respect for cultures, trends, and so on. I also hold great interest in philosophy and cultural anthropology. What's disappointing to me are the strange things that have happened in the cultural arena: these developments are no different from the bizarre use of ultrasonic devices and the shooting up of chicken blood. When it is fashionable, everyone is doing it. When it is over, everyone forgets about it. Being the only one left who still remembers these things is rather lonesome.

After mentioning all these strange things, I should arrive at some sort of a conclusion. In my opinion, tricks are different from genuine knowledge. Knowledge can not only tell you how to do something but also explain why. As for tricks, no one can ever explain why, which is why they are unreliable. There is no trick to make a person smart. But there are plenty of ways to make a person feel smart when in fact they are becoming stupid. A person should remember all the smart things they have done as well as

---

20. The film *Landmine Warfare* (地雷战) was made in 1962 by Tang Yingqi.

all the stupid things—but even more importantly, one should remember how old one is and let go of childish games. With the passing of a new year, I should say something auspicious: hopefully in the new year, we can all avoid strange things and live with integrity—I can't think of anything more auspicious than that.

ODD JOBS

WHILE STUDYING IN THE United States, I did all sorts of odd jobs. One time, it was Old Cao from Shanghai and me taking on a renovation project at a Chinese restaurant. The owner of the restaurant was a Shanghainese monkey-faced scrooge. He had worked as a head chef for most of his life. He had a bit of money saved up, decided to open his own little shop, but thought of himself as some sort of a tycoon—the way he looked at us was unbearable. In the words of Old Cao, he was like a mafia lackey. First day on the job, he said to us: the point of hiring you two is to save money, or else I may as well hire Americans. You must do precisely as I say. You tell me what tools and materials you need and I will buy them. Don't even think about skimming off the top . . .

In the past, I knew that America had advanced technology and advanced commerce but I had no idea that America was also a nation of craftsmen. The street on which we worked was full of them: electricians, plumbers, carpenters, and even contracting firms that took care of entire projects. As soon as they heard about our job, they came over to observe us. When they saw us with our big mallets and hand drills, they smirked and went to the boss in the back to say, "if your two little precious guys can finish renovating this restaurant before the end of the century, I'll give you a hundred bucks." I couldn't hide my anger and nearly threw down the drill in resignation. But Old Cao whispered through the cracks of his teeth: ignore them! If we can't finish the job this century, we still have the next century. Either way the lackey has to pay us . . .

As the old saying goes, without the sharpness of a diamond, don't even think about drilling porcelain. If we took on the gig without knowing how to renovate a house, that was our own shortcoming. Even though I didn't have the skills I could still offer some muscle, enough to qualify as an assistant. Old Cao was from the Hudong Shipyard. He worked his way up from bronze worker to engineer, specializing in ship cabin renovation. Renovating a restaurant was a piece of cake . . . he told me that our most important task was to buy and rent tools, but the lackey boss said, "Don't even think about skimming." Instead of risking being called thieves, it was easier just to make the best of it and earn a couple of bucks.

After demolishing the floor, we earned some amount of respect from the contractors who'd previously insulted us. By the way, we carried the demolished concrete blocks out to the dumpster by hand. The boss didn't even let us rent a wheelbarrow. He thought that having paid for labor, also paying for tools would have been a waste. When the American workers walked by, they would chat with us and tell us how much they admired our spirit. But they added that the way we were going about it wasn't going to get the job done. To be frank, they wanted the job for themselves but couldn't agree to the price. The next step was to take down the old walls. I thought it would be simple to accomplish this so I began swinging the big mallet—after only one swing, the boss told me to stop. He said that I would damage the lumber if I continued to work my way. What sort of lumber could there have been in between the walls? Just a bunch of cheap wood. The boss insisted that it could be used to make the floorboards. As a result, we had to pull the nails out of the rotten wood one by one. When the Americans asked us what we were doing, I told them the truth. They grabbed their bellies and collapsed to the ground, rolling around in laughter. Even Old Cao couldn't keep his cool and blamed me for having a big mouth . . .

After pulling out the nails, we bought some new lumber. The boss wanted to test our carpentry skills so he told us to make a door. Old Cao started sawing the lumber: no matter how I looked at it, the saw didn't seem to work quite right. When it went through the wood, it couldn't help but zigzag. How come it didn't look like any saw that I had ever seen? As we worked, an American carpenter came by. He laughed as he asked what we used to do for a living. Before going abroad, I was a college professor. Of course, I couldn't say that, or it would have brought shame to the school. Old Cao's past was even more of a secret. He couldn't let Hudong Shipyard lose face. I told him that we were artists. It wasn't entirely a lie. Before going abroad, I had published a short story. As for Old Cao, he dabbled in traditional painting, and even had his work shown at the Shanghai Industrial Worker's Art Exhibitions . . . the American replied, "I knew you were artists right away!" I was secretly pleased. We must exude an obvious, recognizable artistic air. But then he added, "No real worker could possibly do what you're doing!" After the American left, Old Cao dropped his saw and cursed.

As it turned out, the saw's real purpose was to prune tree branches in the garden . . .

We worked for our lackey boss for a little over a month and got a few hundred bucks from him, but the restaurant still didn't look like a restaurant. Nor did it look like a cellar—it was more like a pile of trash. In the blink of an eye, the summer gave way to autumn. It was time for us to go back to school. The boss was getting grumpier and grumpier, making us work overtime every day. Rushing us did him no good. With only hand tools and metal pipes in our hands, the job wasn't going to get done for the life of us. The Americans on the street could smell blood and crowded around outside the door waiting for us to make fools of ourselves. At the same time, they were waiting for the boss to turn the job over to them. In a situation like that, even Old Cao couldn't abide it, and finally we quit. The project, like a ripe peach, fell straight into the American workers' hands. Customarily, we should have left as soon as we quit. But Old Cao wanted to see how the Americans worked. He said, the whole project was an embarrassment, but it wasn't his fault. It was all thanks to the old lackey's belly full of brilliant ideas. If we could have done it the way Old Cao wanted, we could have shown the foreigners how the Chinese worked . . .

After the American contractor took over the project, he quickly subcontracted it out to the electrician, the carpenter, and the plumber. You worked in the morning, he worked the afternoon, and tomorrow it will be my turn. In addition to power saws, and power planers, they even had a battery-powered forklift that could drive around inside the building. With the push of a button, they shoved the mess we left behind right out the door. While the electrician got on a power train lift and pulled the wires for the ceiling, the carpenter was down below nailing in the floor. They were pros. Even though they were using prefabricated finishes, you still had to admit they were unimaginably fast. After putting everything in place, they sanded it down with an electric sander and the place sparkled. As soon as they finished, they were out of there. They moved their equipment out and a new crew with new equipment showed up instantly . . . in the blink of an eye, the restaurant started to take shape . . . Old Cao and I watched for a while, then silently slipped away. We had been workers before and knew what it meant to work with dignity.

TALES FROM ABROAD: CLOTHES

WHEN THE EDITORS WROTE to me requesting a series called "Tales from Abroad," I wasn't sure where to start. It reminded me of the part in *The Dream of a Red Chamber* that said, "We didn't participate in any revolutions overseas, didn't catch any criminal masterminds, we were only a couple of poor students for a few years abroad." So I can really only talk about things like clothes, food, lodging, and traveling.

When I first arrived in America, I saw tall buildings, lots of cars, and all sorts of people walking on the streets. As a result, I was troubled by a question that had never occurred to me before: when we went out, what should we wear? For the first month in America, whether it was going to class or meeting with the professor, I was dressed to impress. But after a while, even I began to feel awkward. During class, the whole room was full of people who dressed casually. Some wore baggy pants, some wore T-shirts, and some of the kids who wanted something even airier cut the sleeves off their T-shirts. If you saw someone dressed a bit more formally, this must have been a professor. Once in a while, there was someone who was even more stiffly dressed than the professors. That was the Japanese. The suits the Japanese wore had a particular style that required short limbs and a pair of reading glasses. I could have tried to dress Japanese but first of all, I couldn't pretend to be five feet tall, and second of all, why would I want to dress like them? So in the end, I settled on a casual look.

In America, there were only a few occasions in which you couldn't dress casually, for example—school anniversaries and Thanksgiving parties. On such occasions, ethnic garb proved to be the most appropriate choice. Arab and African guys wore long loose gowns that instantly elicited respect. The Indian and Bangladeshi women wore their colorful saris, elegant and vivacious. The Chinese women could wear their cheongsam, which certainly pleased the eye. But us Chinese men had nothing to wear. I thought about wearing my old blue factory uniform, but regrettably, I didn't bring it with me to America.

One time, there was an Indian who had transferred from Oxford University. Only after seeing him did I understand what statuesque really meant. He was around two meters tall, tied his hair into a topknot, and wore a tight-fitting tunic jacket similar to a Sun Yat-sen suit. No matter where he went, he was always carrying something. He ate as he walked, as if he was the only one around. The American women in our class all found him sexy. Once, during the middle of class, there was a loud crash. Everyone turned around and saw that he had eaten half an apple in one chomp. When he saw everyone looking at him, he raised his apple and said, "May I?" We all felt awkward for looking.

In terms of attire, I wasn't without any success. One winter, when it was snowing, I ran out into the cold wearing a chenille hat, an army-style rain jacket, and a pair of leather boots. People on the street looked at me with a sense of awe. When I got to the bank, a woman even opened the door for me. When I got to school, a Chinese professor I knew said: Mr. Wang, how powerful you are. I quickly looked in a mirror and saw myself looking like a cross between General Patton and a mounted Cossack soldier. But I stopped dressing like that because outside a parking lot, the old security guard kept harassing me, insisting that I trade my hat for his raggedy beanie.

Why is a big man like me talking about clothes? There is a reason.

Clothes were at the heart of a painful experience I had. One summer, with some money on hand, a woman and I went to travel in Europe. We traveled from the south of Europe to the north, and to the streets of Heidelberg. Early one morning by a water fountain, we came across a tour group from mainland China. Seeing our village brethren in a far-off land felt a bit awkward. The dozen or so comrades were crowded together, tightly clutching their briefcases in their right hands as they stared in all directions. They were all dressed in brand-new clothes, it was so clear that they were given a clothing stipend, but it was ugly. First, a big clot of bodies all wearing identical dark brown suits was an unusual sight. Second, their pants were too large, the crotch nearly reached their knees. The translator girl was the only one not wearing those kinds of pants, but her scrunched-up stockings made it look as if she had some sort of skin disease. Furthermore, the Red Army had vanquished the Nazis long ago, what were they so nervous about. The Germans are the kind of people who keep their laughter inside of their bellies. When they saw us, they only revealed a mysterious Mona Lisa smile. It made me so angry, my head hurt.

Were it not for each of our deeply important missions, would any of us have been there to be mocked? But after blaming the foreigners, we also must admit that in the great metropolises of the world, there are people from every sky and every sea. Among them, the Chinese delegations were the biggest eyesores, different from everyone else, weirder than anyone else. It's hard to describe. Even on a Hong Kong street, full of Chinese people, you could instantly spot your mainland second cousin. Of course, clothes are a big part of the problem. It would be nice if something could be done about it.

TALES FROM ABROAD: FOOD

OVERSEAS, I ATE ALL sorts of food, some of it was truly awful. Chinese people who are particular about their food and drink should mentally prepare themselves before going abroad. For example, if an American invites you to eat grilled meat, it will basically be red. After eating it, I wanted to spit my tongue out because I felt like a big bad wolf. As for their raw vegetable salad, it's just a bunch of ripped up lettuce leaves. A venerable elder of the literary community had this to say about it: isn't that for feeding rabbits? Of course, when you stay somewhere long enough, you eventually learn which things are edible. After a year or two in America, one quickly learns that the hamburgers and fried chicken sold at fast-food restaurants are things that we can eat. A pizza pie sold in America is also not a problem. But outside of America, we're in for another surprise. I ate a rice salad while traveling in France. When I realized that the rice was raw and sour, I couldn't swallow it. In Italy, I tried their pizza and found it too sour and fishy. Even though it was still edible, the flavor was all wrong. The highlight of a pizza, that layer of melted cheese, was completely missing. All that was left was the tomato sauce and a couple of anchovies. Then, we went to eat at a Chinese restaurant. Outside the town of Cambridge, I got a plate of fried rice. That was a truly hard-hitting dish. Later when I mentioned the rice in a letter to my older brother, I said it could be loaded into a hunting rifle and used to hunt mallards. Even though these restaurants had Chinese signs, you couldn't find a single Chinese person in them.

But there's more. Not far from where I lived in America, there was a restaurant called Bamboo Garden, which was under constantly changing management. For a while, the owner was Thai. When a Burmese owner took over, it was still called Bamboo Garden, but they no longer used oil to fry the dishes, only water. When I find these sorts of places in America, I take care to avoid them. Of course, if one were to say that I was starving in Europe, that wouldn't be true either. Eventually, I bought a few kilos of roast meat and washed it down with beer, which left me drunk all day long. Upon returning to America from Europe, I had already lost quite a bit of weight. The corners of my mouth were inflamed, probably due to the vitamin deficiency of my diet. Chinese people never travel without a couple of bags of instant noodles in their backpacks. A friend once told to me that, had it not been for instant noodles, he would have starved on his train ride from Beijing to Moscow.

As far as I can tell, if Confucius were to go abroad today, he would starve to death. The old man wouldn't eat any meat that's not cut straight. The meat Americans grill up isn't even cut; you have to cut it yourself, on the table. But the knives they use are as light as a feather. Trying to cut straight with them is nearly impossible. The old man also said that every meal should be paired with the appropriate sauce. Near where I lived, there was a Chinese restaurant called Peking Pavilion where they sold Peking duck. You want to know what sauce they put on the Peking duck? Strawberry jam. They also dipped spring rolls in applesauce. But even with such enigmatic pairings, the foreigners still said it was delicious.

If Confucius wanted to go abroad, unless he took a personal chef with him, he would have to learn to eat ketchup. That's the best sauce Americans have come up with. This ketchup is for putting on hamburgers. It comes in little plastic packets. There are a ton of them at McDonald's, and the packets are all free. Every time I go there to eat, I grab a big handful to put on other things when I got home. The old man would also have to eat meat that isn't cut straight because American knives don't have sharp edges—maybe it's because they are worried it might hurt someone—so the meat will always come out jagged.

Suppose Chinese people weren't as insistent about dicing everything into small pieces, or making sure everything is fully cooked, or seasoning everything just right, then they could go anywhere. Furthermore, they could also end up with fat heads and big ears, with backs of tigers and waists of bears. Of course, in those places where chicken wings are cheaper than a cabbage, anyone would put on some extra meat. When I was there, I weighed 90 kilos, but it was still nothing. No matter what season it was, there were usually Black men out and about wearing tank tops, showing off their muscles. You had to believe that they were just guys who loved to exercise or else you might feel intimidated.

Suppose you thought that raw meat and raw vegetables were only meant to be eaten by young people, and not the old, then you would be wrong. One of my neighbors was an old man, a commercial illustrator. His beard was black and slick. He ran around wearing tight jeans and whenever he came across a pretty young lady, he would offer her a bit of flattery. Later he told me that he was seventy years old. In my class, there was also a seventy-five-year-old American lady, full of life. You could see her everywhere. Once, I went to the school choir's rehearsal. She stood in the middle of the front row. But that day, she walked off the stage holding her mouth. As it turns out, when she hit the high note of the aria, her dentures fell out and ended up next to someone in the third row. In any case, old people in America are full of energy. My parents are no match for them.

Suppose you said that culinary skills didn't determine everything, and that what you ate mattered just as much—I would have to agree. Besides, exercise is just as important to health. In the half year before returning home, I also worked out. I jogged under the full sun and did push-ups in the park. As a result, after I returned, I looked tanned and beefy compared to the department chiefs and old professors who were only there for short surveys and training programs (those who go on long trips mostly don't return). When I was at border customs, they made me wait until everyone else had passed. They even lectured me about not showing any discipline during my official outing abroad. At the time, this pissed me off. Nowadays, I only eat the finest, most delicate foods. And after avoiding sun and exercise for three years, I finally look like an intellectual again.

TALES FROM ABROAD: HOUSING

P　**EOPLE ALL LIVE IN INDOORS,** it is our unchanging way. Different types of people live in different types of housing. Unfortunately, not everyone has reached this profound understanding. This is because homes are built by people, and people live in them. In America, some people live in apartments, and some people live in houses, two very different types of housing. Apartments are tall buildings in the city; they are similar to our public housing units. What is different about them is that they have red carpets in the hallways and a concierge sitting in the lobby. In even nicer buildings—for example, the ones on New York's Fifth Avenue—there is even a dapper old man in a red uniform standing by the front door who opens car doors for visitors. I've never been inside those places because I don't know anyone who lives there.

Judging by their cars, they must be wealthy individuals. Then, there are courtyard tennis courts and rooftop pools. It doesn't imply anything other than that they have money. The people who built the buildings have money, and the people who live in them have even more money. This thing, money, we'll soon have as well, of this I am fairly certain. Furthermore, on these apartment patios, there usually aren't piles of garbage—pieces of wood, old cardboard, old chimney pipes, etcetera—, what this implies I am not sure. One time, a French girl I knew pointed to an apartment patio in Beijing and remarked on the weathered piles of rubbish: Beijing is a big city, and these buildings are pretty decent. Don't the people who live there have any sense of pride? Why do they make their houses look like slums? I didn't have the heart to burst her bubble.

Speaking of apartments, I am reminded of the buildings at the heart of downtown Paris. Those buildings weren't necessarily apartments, but they looked like apartments. They were built with light-gray stone blocks, slate roof tiles, and wrought iron window beams. In front of them were cobblestone streets. It's hard to say exactly what was good about them, but they were nice to look at. With the stones, you can say that Paris is an ancient city, a peerless garden metropolis. Beijing was once a peerless ancient metropolis as well. Its charm came from its city walls. In America, I ran into an old missionary who had lived in China for many years. He began asking me about Beijing's walls the moment he saw me. When I said they had been taken down, he looked like he wanted to die.

As for houses, these are usually one- or two-story buildings in the suburbs and countryside. Inside of a house usually lives a family, so the word *house* is similar to our idea of "home." But without the walls, I can guarantee you that if you had a verdant lawn and a couple of big trees, you would hate having a courtyard wall too. Not only would it block other people's view of your flora, but it would ruin your own scenery as well. A few mud puddles and piglets certainly cannot be considered scenery. Better to keep those out of sight. But I've never seen mud puddles or piglets anywhere near foreign houses. Of course, those things exist everywhere, but Europeans and Americans don't like to have them appear near the house. If my understanding of the situation is correct, the word *house* should really be translated into "garden-home." Aside from the house itself, it also includes the open environment. The few who build courtyard walls there are usually country bumpkins with too much money.

Every American house must have a lawn. Some can be as large a hundred acres and some can be as small as just a few square yards. But the big ones come with a price. The lawn must be mowed. One of our neighbors was too lazy to do it, so he ended up mulching the ground with tree bark and planting a couple of fern pines. It didn't look bad at all, sort of a forest vibe. No one ever cuts off all the grass leaving only bare soil because that would turn into mud in the rain. When people have to move the earth to build a new house, they first cover the earth with pebbles. After all, next door is someone else's house.

Some people have houses with ponds and other people have houses with big lakes. You can drink the water from these lakes without even disinfecting it. But here, I'm going off on a tangent. In America, there are also places where land is so scarce that they build on hills. But when they do it, they don't touch the trees or the grass on the hills. They just stick the house right on the side of the hill. As a result, the hill is still the same hill, and the trees are still the same trees. The hills and trees belong to people, birds, and beasts alike. It's not like here where we make a mess and make everything look like a mass grave. Their situation doesn't have too much to do with wealth inequality. It's mostly just a matter of where you want to live. On a side note, in most places in America, seeing squirrels on the windowsill is completely normal.

But in terms of loving their homes and private gardens, Americans are barely even worth mentioning. The Europeans put even more thought into their homes. The best garden-homes in the world are near Austria's mountainous Salzburg region, according to van Loon. I think what he says is reasonable. The people who built those houses aren't wealthy, just a couple of mountain farmers. When I went to visit, I saw houses in the middle of mature woods. I can't get into details about the houses here because my heart itches at the very thought of them. It makes me want to go to Austria and take the houses along with the woods back home with me. All I can say is this: in the woods, I saw a small path going to a farmer's home. The path was paved with a type of pebble stones that never gets dusty. Had that path been paved with stone slabs or some other material, it wouldn't have looked as good. But I also think that the ranches in Holland with their windmills, dykes, canals, etcetera, are also beautiful garden-homes, on par with the Austrian homes. Heidelberg, Germany, is on the banks of the river Neckar. On the river is a magnificent bridge. A foreign poet once wrote: O, old bridge, how many times have you carried me! Had he wanted show more passion, he would have to have died on the bridge. Near Cambridge, there is a Byron Pond. Even though it's just a little pond in the wilderness, it's still the place where a century ago, Lord Byron jumped in for a swim. Since then, not a single blade of grass has gone missing. Surrounded by green grass and ancient woods, a person cannot help but feel the love that the inhabitants of the place feel for their environment. You wouldn't dare to throw a tin can on the ground. And the people living there will continue to love every blade of grass and every tree. Every puddle of mud they turn, every stone they move, they do with utmost care. People who don't love their homes can hardly be considered people, and the home doesn't just refer to the space behind the door.

TALES FROM ABROAD: TRAVEL

WHEN WE (MY WIFE AND I) were studying in America, we took a trip to Europe one year. This required ordering round-trip tickets between America and Europe, as well as European train tickets. This process sounds complicated but in reality, it was a breeze. We went to our school's travel agency and expressed our needs. A young lady picked up the telephone and asked us, "You wanted the cheapest tickets, right?" Then, after a few phone calls, everything was arranged. We departed on Kuwait Airways and returned on America's People Express. In Europe, we used Eurail passes. All we had to do was to arrive at certain travel agencies in Europe and America to pick up our tickets and we could travel to over a dozen countries for a month. And this was the most complicated way of arranging travels. Had we had a credit card, we wouldn't even have had to go to the school's travel agency. We could have just made a few phone calls from home and it would have been done. This was six or seven years ago, but I assume it is still the same now.

Recently, my wife went to Africa to attend an international conference—as for what conference or what country specifically, I won't mention it here. The topic of the conference was very important, the attendees were all high-level scholars and activists. From this perspective, the conference was very high quality, however its organization not so much. For my wife, it was difficult to even get to there. This was because the round-trip plane tickets were all arranged by the conference organizers. They sent us a fax detailing the departure time, port of transfer, etc., but did not reveal on which airline. When she called the conference organizers, no one answered. As a result, she had to go to every airline in Beijing to ask if there was such a route. Of course, the most probable were the African airlines, but nothing came of it. She tried to call and fax the conference organizers again, but still no one answered. Given such a situation, the fact that she was able to appear at the conference at all was pure serendipity.

After returning from Africa, she explained to me what the phone situation there was like: there were telephones in some places—for example, where their conference was held—the university had one phone at their gatehouse. Suppose someone wanted to call a representative, theoretically someone was supposed to run out of the gatehouse, go to the dormitory, look for the representative, and tell her to pick up the phone. The whole process should have taken an hour, and for the whole time, the caller would have had to stay on the line. Suppose it was an international call, the phone bill would have been astronomical. In reality, there was no one at the gatehouse taking calls, so such a process would not even have occurred. Furthermore, faxes sent out of Africa show up like ants forming a pattern in the sky, difficult to decipher. And faxes going into Africa turned out the same way. This made it practically impossible to contact people, which had its pros and cons. Pro, you never get woken up at five o'clock in the morning with a phone call that you had to pay for. It might have been a student on vacation telling you that they forgot to turn in their dissertation or forgot to pay their tuition, in any case, you would have had to run the errand for them; con, there was no way for outsiders to do business with them. My wife said, even though the place was a national capital, there was no industry or commerce, only a big farmer's market. To me, that wasn't too surprising.

As for the plane ticket, the situation went like this: the organizers ordered a ticket for my wife, but booked it along with another person, under this other person's name. That was why she couldn't get any information on it.

Considering the reality of more than a billion people in China, the fact that my wife eventually got her ticket and ended up in Africa was a miracle. After she arrived, she spent a part of her time at the conference and a part of her time running around trying to get hold of her return ticket. The staff at the conference were very amiable African aunties and uncles. No matter who you asked, they would refer you to someone else.

The people who worked at the airport would always say, come back tomorrow, I'm sure everything will be resolved by then. All these aunties and uncles were working hard, drenched in sweat. The representatives from OSPAAAL[21] were also drenched in sweat. I don't know how she eventually managed to come back. Neither does she. As a scholar and author, all these experiences are meaningful. If necessary, she would travel to that country again. But had she been a businesswoman for whom time was money, I'm afraid that would not have been her position.

---

21. Organization of Solidarity with the People of Asia, Africa, and Latin America

My wife learned an African phrase. I'm not sure what country it was from, but all the African can understand it, "Ayayaya!" which apparently means, advance, progress. "Ayayaya Afriaca" means: Africa, advance. At night, when everyone danced the traditional dance, that's what they would shout it. Indeed, ayayaya was called for. The state of travel and communication in our country is perhaps somewhat better than in East African countries. But compared to the developed world standard, we are still far behind. Let us also shout: Ayayaya, China!

TALES FROM ABROAD: THIEVES

WHEN TRAVELING ABROAD, coming across robbers is the most unpleasant experience. Even though Pittsburgh is considered a relatively safe city, there were still quite a few unsavory characters lurking in the shadows, so it was common to read about robberies in the newspaper. The odd thing was, in the first two years at school, we never heard about any Chinese people being robbed. According to reliable sources, we were under the protection of Bruce Lee. Even though this brother had passed away a few years prior, his kung fu movies were still being shown.

Anyone could understand Bruce Lee's power—on the silver screen, he always let out a strange yelp before busting out a high kick. When those bad guys with criminal intent saw this, they chewed on their nails and thought, "Holy crap! Against a kick like that, even a gun wouldn't work." Foreigners see us just like how we see them: you're either black, or white, or yellow, anything more subtle is hard to notice. As far as they can tell, we are all Bruce Lees.

But the situation quickly changed. It started with the 1984 National Day celebration. All the Chinese overseas students got together in the school's auditorium and made dumplings and spring rolls to share with the Americans. After the meal, they cordially invited us to give a performance. A courageous fellow from the engineering school volunteered. He got on stage and performed a set of "beginner's long fist style" and explained that it was Chinese kung fu. I noticed in the audience a couple of Black guys whispering to each other, looking unimpressed. This was an omen that something unfortunate was going to happen, and so it happened.

There were about seven or eight Chinese people in our building. The first to be robbed was Young Song from downstairs. This fellow student was unlike the rest of us. During the 1977 college entrance exam,[22] he had been admitted by two schools. One was the Chengdu Athletics Academy and the other was the Northeastern Engineering School. In the end, he chose the engineering school but he was fully qualified to become an athlete. For that reason, he was rather arrogant.

To get to the department to make experiments at night, he could have driven a car, but he insisted on walking. He had to cross a large lawn in the dark, and the lawn was surrounded by dense woods. We all told him to be careful, but he said he wasn't scared. Even if he couldn't win a fight, he could run. This friend of ours could run a hundred-meter dash in eleven seconds, most people couldn't catch up. One night, when he returned home at around 1:00 a.m., he said he had been robbed. There were two robbers, one was tall, and one was short. The place where he was robbed was

---

22. In 1977, Deng Xiaoping officially reinstalled the national university entrance exams based on academic knowledge. This practice had been interrupted during the Cultural Revolution.

close to our home, so the bandits couldn't have gone far. There were four or five guys in our building, and the news made us furious. We decided to go out there for a little payback. We even found a baseball bat and wanted to take it with us. Just before going out the door, I asked Young Song, "You run fast, why didn't you run?"

He said the tall one had a gun in his hand. Even though he added that the gun didn't look real, everyone still thought it wasn't worth the risk. Not only that, but they blamed Young Song for not mentioning the gun earlier. Our families were thousands of miles away, and we were their hopes and dreams, we could not let anything happen to ourselves.

A few days later, I was robbed too. There was only one bandit and he didn't carry a gun. He was a white boy, shorter and skinnier than me, and a bit sickly looking. Theoretically, it should have been me robbing him, but well, I was the one getting robbed. The only explanation for this turn of events was that I was unconscious for their duration. I was robbed at the break of dawn, on my way to get some exercise in the park. The park was in a small valley, past a long wooden handrail. That's where I ran into him. He said to me, "Dude, give me some money." I replied, "I didn't bring any money." He said, "Let me look in your wallet." (Asshole! What right do you have to look in my wallet?) I replied, "I didn't bring a wallet." He said, "Then what's that thing bulging out of your pocket?" (As if, what business is it of yours?) I said, "It's a packet of cigarettes." He said, "I was just about to ask you for a smoke." So I gave him a cigarette. He took the opportunity to look in my pocket; there was indeed no wallet. After parting, I ran for about a hundred meters before realizing that I was the victim of an attempted robbery. And by the way, only later did I think of the words in the parentheses. At the time, I was so fat that I couldn't wear any of my belts, I needed to run to lose some weight, and my mind was preoccupied. But of course, if I you were to insist that I was scared and didn't have the guts to talk back, I would also have to accept that. Later I learned that people sold drugs in that park. The guy I came across was most likely in need of something, looking for money to buy some weed to take the edge off. Some people say that when you come across addicts, it's better to give them some money or else they might stab or bite you. I figured this wasn't something to play around with, so then I always walked around the park.

For a period after that, the criminals of Pittsburgh kept robbing Chinese people because they had heard that because Chinese students didn't have credits cards, preferring instead to carry lots of cash. People were getting robbed increasingly often. When this one guy from the engineering school got robbed, he tried to reason with the thief, talking about dreams and humanity, hoping to work on the guy on an emotional level. As a result, he was punched in the face, leaving his eyes and mouth slanted. But those guys never robbed girls, which meant that at least they were honorable thieves. But then there was an exception. It was Young Xia, from the medical school. She was the prettiest flower in all of Pittsburgh, the pride of the Chinese community. In other words, she was gorgeous. According to her, this is what happened: at around eleven o'clock at night, she and her husband had just come out of the movie theater and were waiting for the bus. Suddenly, three big brutes jumped out of nowhere, flashed their handguns, and shouted, "This is a robbery!" Then they asked for their wallets. After looking through the wallets and taking all their cash, the bus arrived. The three bandits waved their guns in the air and got on the bus—under such circumstances, our friends had no interest in sharing the same bus so they waited for the next one home. According to this narrative, they had no choice but to be robbed. The husband was a nerdy looking student, no match for three big Black brutes. Besides, their opponents had guns. Even if he had been Mu Tiezhu the basketball player, a gunshot would have left his health in jeopardy.

But there was another version of the story. At the time, another

Chinese student was waiting for a bus at a different stop not far from them. According to him, the story went like this: at around eleven o'clock at night, the moviegoers had dispersed, there wasn't a soul on the street. As Young Xia and her husband were waiting for the bus, so were three big brutes, but they weren't hiding in the dark. The three looked a bit thuggish, but they weren't wielding handguns. One of them carried a big thing on his shoulder, but it wasn't a semiautomatic rifle, nor a bazooka, but a boom box. The three of them were singing and shimmying but Young Xia and her husband weren't catching the groove at all. You could hear their teeth chattering from across the street. I imagine this must have had something to do with all the robberies happening at the time, and the fact that the bus refused to show up on time. In any case, some time passed and the couple began to discuss: should we ask them? Another moment passed. Better to ask, all right. So Young Xia went up to the Black brother and asked, "May I ask if you plan on robbing us?" The guy froze for a moment, then put on a sinister grin, "That's right, we're here to rob you!" Young Xia said, "Then you must want to look through our wallets?" The guy started to snicker, "True, true, gimme your wallets!"

Young Xia said, "Here are the wallets." The guys took the wallets, and after returning the wallets, said, "Thank you!" Before shimmying off somewhere to get a drink. Of the two stories, I'm more inclined to believe the latter because the police station was right next to the movie theater. When the cops couldn't find anywhere to park, they parked on the movie theater lot. American policemen always carry a gun on their hip. Had anyone tried to commit a robbery there, the assailant would have caught a bullet from a pug-nosed revolver. But if you insisted on offering money to them, of course they wouldn't refuse. I imagined that after these sorts of experiences, we had not only gotten a reputation for carrying cash, but also for being easy to rob. I predicted more and more robberies, and maybe all the thieves in America would swarm to Pittsburgh.

However, after that people stopped talking about robberies, which was strange. Among the Chinese overseas students in Pittsburgh, there was an Old Jing. The difference between this old brother and the rest of us was that he was a lifelong learner, much older than the rest of us. When he heard about people getting robbed he said, "You youngsters ain't nothing!" In addition, he was ethnically Korean so he also added, "You Han students are cowards, you're encouraging the problem. If it were me, money I don't got, but I got the fight to death!" His words made us rather uncomfortable, but none of us wanted to talk back to him. Old Jing had his one moment of glory. When he was traveling in Europe, he came across a knife-wielding bandit. He armed himself with his camera tripod and battled until the bandit fled. But that one story wasn't enough to impress anyone. I can't say that I was hoping for him to undergo the danger of an encounter with a bandit. But suppose he did come across one, I hoped that Old Jing could stand before the bandit's gun and set a good example for us "youngsters." One day, someone saw Old Jing in front of a supermarket, hands shaking, lips mumbling, completely out of sorts.

Someone helped him to his car and sat him down. He opened a can of Coca-Cola and offered him a drink. After asking what had happened, it turned out that Old Jing had been robbed. But the situation wasn't quite what I had hoped it to be. At the time, he was shopping. He was thirsty so he went to the automatic vending machine and purchased a can of Coke. It was in a tight corner. After hearing a loud *bang*, a bandit jumped out from behind the vending machine. It was a little Black boy, maybe twelve years of age, holding a tiny screwdriver in his hand. He pointed it at Old Jing and mewed, "Robbery! Your money!" Old Jing lost his mind and heard himself shriek, "Asshole! Get your ass home!" The kid bawled and ran off. After scaring away the bandit, Old Jing was still furious like a mad goat.

Later, the Pittsburgh police caught two bandits. They held a press conference at the school and there were no more cases after that. The two bandits were the two guys who had initially robbed Young Song. Everyone who had been robbed said it was those two guys, but I didn't believe it. At least personally, I wasn't robbed by those two. Nowadays, it is my understanding that during our time in this world, we have two important responsibilities. One is to be a good person, so as to not waste our one precious life. To this end, I'm still way off. The other is to not encourage other people's bad habits. To this end, I'm even further off. If fact, we all are. Take for example where I live (I returned to China long ago), there is a road right in front of our door. All the gutter covers have been stolen from it. This is a bad habit that we have all allowed to take hold.

TALES FROM ABROAD: FARM

ANYWHERE WHERE THERE ARE Chinese people, there are Chinese restaurants; the restaurant industry is a reliable source of livelihood for Chinese immigrants. In the past, most of the Chinese in America all had something to do with restaurants. That is no longer the case. Now, some people might be software engineers, some might be teachers, but the number of options is still quite limited. In the study of physics, there are four forces: the strong force, the weak force, the electromagnetic force, and gravity. Abroad, Chinese people hold the same positions, more or less. However, it must be noted that the vast majority of mainland Chinese work as farmers but, in America, Chinese people rarely work on farms. This is because by local standards, the Chinese don't know how to farm. When I first arrived in America, I met an old

America lady named Wolf, as in Big Bad Wolf. She was a farmer, but she wanted to quit. She asked me to teach her Chinese so that she could go to China to teach. I was to teach her Chinese and she was to teach me English, because she couldn't afford to pay tuition. In this deal, I got the short end of the bargain. I taught her quite a few local Beijing sayings, whereas she pulled out a volume of Milton and told me to recite it out loud. The more I read, the less I knew how to talk. Mrs. Wolf had a degree in Anglo-American literature, but when the words she taught me came out of my mouth, people laughed. That isn't to say that there was some flaw in her education. It only shows how the times have changed. In a newspaper, I read an opinion piece by a Harvard English department professor titled "On *Midsummer Night's Dream*." Students no longer read Shakespeare's plays, but instead rented videotapes of Shakespeare performances. The girls in the video all wore short skirts and there were even laser beams. Mrs. Wolf asked me to read Yang Wan-li's poems to her. Afterward, she shook her head and said it didn't sound like poetry. I understand that reading ancient poems requires a certain sort of elocution, but I'm not some old medieval fogey, how would I know how to do that. I didn't think this old lady's understanding of language made her a good candidate to come teach English in China. In the end, she never came.

Now let's talk about Mrs. Wolf's livelihood—not long after meeting her, she invited me to her farm, driving me there personally. After a four-hour drive out of the city, we were surrounded by lush fields. She said to me, not counting the woods and the house, there were a hundred acres of pasture. When I first arrived, a dog made an appearance, then quickly returned to watch the sheep. Mrs. Wolf said she could sell the farm. This is to say that she could sell the land, the flock, and the dog, and walk away, that was all doable. But the dog couldn't sell the farm—in other words, if the dog had wanted to sell the land, the flock, and Mrs. Wolf to someone else, and walk away, that wasn't doable because Mrs. Wolf couldn't watch the flock. The conclusion of the joke is that the farm could run without her, but not without the dog. Of course, the old lady was just being self-deprecating. When we got to the farm, she said: got to gas up the car, if you forget before going out, there are no gas stations around. So she parked the car next to a big oil tank and used a hand pump to fill up the gas tank. She pumped as swiftly as the wind. I helped her pump for a bit, but I couldn't do it as quickly, and it was exhausting. The old lady was short and thin, around sixty years of age. I was a hulk of a man, and only thirty-five years old. But I must admit, my arm wasn't as strong as hers. She told me that she used to keep oil barrels out in the open, but the neighbors complained about it being ugly. Local authorities came and said it was unsafe. So, in the end, she had to build an underground oil tank where she could keep a few tons of gas. My first reaction was that she was exaggerating: even if she was able to mix the concrete, how did she dig up all that dirt by herself. I didn't voice my suspicions. After all, Old Lady Wolf's arm was like an iron bar. Later, she took me to go look at her things—tractor, lawn mower, and so on. With all that machinery, it must take her a lot of work to maintain, not to mention repair. It must have been a nightmare. I asked her if she hired people to fix the machines when they broke down. She straight up yelled: hire someone? With what money?

Only later did I understand that Mrs. Wolf's attitude toward farming was that of a hobbyist. Even though she had a degree in agronomy, and was as hardworking as could be, in the end, she was still an old lady. As a truly independent laborer, when your machine brakes, sending it to be fixed by others is shameful. Not only are you giving other people your hard-earned money, but it also proved your own ineptitude. Later, we visited the home of a crane operator. What he took pride in wasn't his three-hundred-thousand-dollar crane but all his tools and hardware. Those things came in sets of hundreds. Of course, I couldn't make heads or tails of them. He explained, operating a crane couldn't really be considered a skill, the real skill lies in knowing how to repair them. When a neighbor or colleague needed something repaired and asked him for help, he felt honored. But when he couldn't fix his own broken gear and had to ask someone for help, it always felt awkward. In any case, that was his livelihood. He was good at what he did, so he always walked tall. After all those years in America, these things rubbed off on me. On the computer I use to write my books, I wrote the software myself. When the machine breaks, I don't ask for help but try to tinker with it myself. This way of doing things can certainly cultivate a sense of self-esteem.

Old Lady Wolf had three daughters. The oldest one was pretty successful, a representative of some big corporation stationed in Japan. This daughter invited her to stay with her, but she had refused. She didn't think it seemed interesting. In her house I saw a man's sock. In our conversations, she had mentioned something about her sex life. But she didn't live with anyone else. According to her, a person and a dog on a farm is the ideal way of life. But she also admitted that in recent years, it was getting hard to keep up. First of all, she had to sheer two thousand sheep. That amount of work could kill you. And then, she had to bale hay in the fall. In addition, surrounding her pasture was more than ten kilometers of electric fence to keep the wolves out (more accurately, North American coyotes), and to keep the sheep in. If any part of it broke, it had to be fixed immediately or else it would have been a disaster. When all the work was done, she was exhausted. At the time, it was late autumn. On her property, there were a dozen perfectly good apple trees, but the apples had all fallen on the ground. She also planted some potatoes, but for some reason, they grew out of the soil. We had a few for dinner and they tasted like Sichuan peppers—numbingly spicy. I wondered if she hadn't planted them wrong—potatoes shouldn't taste like that. As I gazed out, I spotted a few white dots in the lush green pasture. Upon closer inspection, they were dead sheep. Their horns were still intact, but their wool had already been washed away by the rain. They had probably been dead for a while. The old lady's face showed deep regret as she looked at the dead sheep. She said: should've slaughtered the old sheep and skinned their hides. Old sheep hide could still be of some use but she couldn't get around to slaughtering them all. Besides, she wasn't even sure how many sheep she had. The sheep there not only died of their own accord but were also born of their own volition. Only Candy (her dog) knew. When Candy heard its name, it barked and wagged its tail. Such was what I witnessed at Old Lady Wolf's farm.

In America, I met quite a few people like Mrs. Wolf—a crane operator, a restaurant owner, a small-town dentist—most of them steadily stuck with a livelihood, some with more success than others. The less successful ones wanted to switch to a different livelihood. None of them played in the stock market or tried to write some story to capture the world's attention. It would be appropriate to call these the people. When American politicians bring up the reason for America's wealth and strength, they always give primary credits to America's hardworking people rather than crediting themselves for their correct leadership. Back in China, I also met people like these. As for those people who can play the market, or those who can write cutting edge theoretical essays, I'm in less of a hurry to get to know. Perhaps this is only natural.

TALES FROM ABROAD: CHINESE RESTAURANTS

DURING MY SECOND YEAR studying in America, I had to write a term paper for my anthropology class. The professor told us to study a group of people, and to tell a story. I said to the professor, I want to study Cantonese people. He said that wasn't a good idea, I wasn't Cantonese. He said there were quite a few Chinese people working in restaurants, why not write about them. At first, I wasn't interested, but after thinking it over, I figured I may as well take a look. I worked at a restaurant for two months. The boss was named Whip Cracker Zhou. Later, the boss and I had a fight and I walked out. My paper received several As. The professor was named Singleton. He was once the chairman of the American Anthropological Association. All this digression is to explain that I worked at the restaurant for the purpose of research, not for making money. With that said, we can return to the topic at hand. The restaurant where I worked was called Kitchen X. I washed dishes in the kitchen. At the time, business was booming. They hired three chefs. The head chef cooked, the sous chef verbally abused the line cook, and the line cook spent all day moaning. Later, the line cook and I became fairly close. We were kind of best friends. The guy was around fifty years old back then, always drinking, always sloppy. He had been in America for almost twenty years, but he couldn't speak a word of English. His is the story of a Pittsburgh man. Pittsburgh isn't Manhattan. Here, machismo is an important cultural value. So his story isn't of the romantic kind. Not only isn't it romantic, but it's rather tragic. The line cook is named Li, hailing from Shandong. When he was young, he was conscripted into the Nationalist Army, where he was eventually dragged to Taiwan. In the army, he worked his way up to the rank of chief of staff.

Kitchen X had a strange layout. There were twists and turns as soon as you went in. First you had to turn left, then right. It was like the inside of an intestine. But the place wasn't small, it could fit up to forty tables, and it was decent. The interior designer must have been a master to be able to create such a hedge maze grotto. My friend said that the place used to be a rundown warehouse. First, they closed off the entrance and made it into a spring roll stand. There weren't any tables yet. After operating for a few years, they made some money and renovated another small space so they could start selling stir-fry. A few years later, they renovated some more. The twists and turns were there to hide the mess left behind. Had people been able to see the old, dilapidated walls, who would have wanted to eat there? In the deep of winter, they sold spring rolls on the street, breaths billowing like smoke; after stir-frying all day, they became carpenters and masons at night. It wasn't pleasant. That's why calling it a hedge maze grotto wasn't as accurate as calling it a vermiculated wormhole. The restaurant was the product of the boss's ten years of bootstrapping. He had endured true hardship. On the other hand, who didn't endure hardship trying to start a business in America. My friend also said, he didn't mind hardship but his whole life involved just a bit too much of it. In the past, after being discharged from the army, he opened a little shop in Taipei. His life wasn't that bad, but one day an old customer came to him and said let's try to make it big in New York City, we'll be rich. I'll take care of the green card for you. So my friend got a tourist visa and was on his way. After getting off the plane in New York, before he even had had time to get over his jet lag, he started cooking. The guy said to him: don't even think about going outside! The immigration police are looking for people just like you. From there, he cooked all day, watched the shop at night, and in the blink of an eye, more than ten years had passed. Not only did he never go out; he hardly even saw the sun.

At this point in the story, it should be clear that this Kitchen X was his own establishment. As for how he got from New York to here, it's not hard to guess. After working in New York for over a decade, the guy gave him a green card and said, hey, it came through, we're even. We Shandong people understand gratitude, but we're not stupid. Trading over a decade of blood and sweat for a piece of paper is a bad deal. He couldn't possibly have worked another day for that man-faced beast, he needed to forge his own path. There were too many Chinese restaurants in New York; the competition was too stiff, so he came to Pittsburgh. Here, he became the head chef. He was his own boss.

As for me, I have not had a chance to introduce myself. I was sent to a commune, served in the army corps, worked in a factory, I've done everything. As far as I can tell, working as a chef in America is the most exhausting work you can do. For him to make a couple of dishes, he had to arrive at the restaurant a little past nine, clean the kitchen, prepare the raw ingredients, and after a long hustle, he could start stir-frying at ten. After cooking until one o'clock at night, he cleaned up, cooked the workers a meal, and finished just after two. And that would have been on a good day. Suppose a couple of customers sat there and refused to leave, you couldn't very well kick them out. At most, you could ask a few times: sir, is there anything else you would like to order? And that could easily go on to four in the morning. And if the sanitation department came for an inspection, it would have been an all-night battle. And the sanitation department always came, so you had to get on your knees and scrub the grease under the stove with a stainless-steel scrubber. By my estimates, these chefs worked fifteen hours a day in front of the smoky, oily flame, and they didn't even get Sundays off. If you worked for a boss, at least you could ask for a few days off every month. Working for yourself, there was none of that. Although outside there is a beautiful world, you never have time to even look. Meanwhile, things like life or youth simply vanish like a wisp of smoke. Suffering like that must have been for a valid reason. Kitchen X had three chefs. The head chef was nearly seventy years old. He wasn't saving money for his son but for his grandson's tuition. At the mention of his litter of grandchildren, he swelled with pride. The sous chef would endure each month so that on his day off, he would cruise straight to the casinos in New Jersey and not return until having lost all his money. Granted, a life like that is not completely without excitement. But this best friend of mine, formerly known as Boss Li, even he didn't know what he was working for.

Boss Li said, when he came to start his business in Pittsburgh, he was thirtysomething years old, single, with no parents above him or children below. He had endured hardship all his life, so he didn't mind hard work. It all sounded a bit strange. Where had he learned to be so high-minded? Another thing I didn't understand was, how had he managed to open a restaurant without having learned English? At this point in the story, my guy stuttered a bit. As it turns out, he had started the restaurant with an Italian woman.

For a while, he could even speak a little Italian, which he had learned back in New York. New York's Chinatown is right next to Little Italy. For a Chinese chef to have known an Italian woman wasn't all that strange. For some reason, the woman decided to elope with him. There's something slightly romantic about that part of the story. After arriving in Pittsburgh, my friend used his life's savings and the tenacity of a suckling babe to open shop. The woman worked the cash register. It turned out that love was what fueled his entrepreneurial spirit. He had finally gotten a taste of that foreign goodness. My good friend added, don't ask me any more questions, women are all poisonous snakes, they take everything they can get.

As for Italy, I know a thing or two about it. Italy is beautiful and Italian girls are gorgeous. When we traveled in Italy, our cameras and wallets were stolen. After reporting to the Italian police, they said, if they're gone, they're gone, other than you foreign tourists, who else is there to steal from. When our overseas compatriot Yang Chuang-kwan went to Rome for the Olympics, he should have gotten a gold metal but ended up losing his virgin powers to an Italian girl. He only ended up with a bronze medal, and the gold medal went to some Italian guy. This story shows that the Italians are masters of the honey trap. Yang Chuang-kwan was an unparalleled talent in the history of Chinese athletics, nicknamed "Decathlon Iron Man," but even he was defeated, not to mention little old Boss Li. Boss Li said that at first the Italian woman had been good to him, sweetheart this and sweatheart that. This might very well have been true. As we all know, Chinese food tastes good but the kitchens stink. After a day of stir-frying, his body was covered in an oily stench that never fully washed off. Furthermore, after a lifetime in American kitchens, his face was a mawkish yellow, like dried sugarcane peel. I have a strong suspicion that cooking oil reacts with facial skin, resulting in a dark yellow organic compound. On top of that, after eighteen hours in the kitchen, he was probably useless in bed. Even if there were some romantic feelings, it wouldn't have counted for much. Even though business was good, he saw very little cash. At times, he was so short on cash that he had to buy discount vegetables. Working in the restaurant business in America, this had been a major faux pas. A single rotten leaf can shut down a whole operation. It's not like the eateries in Beijing where whenever a migrant worker shows up, the chef throws the fat and offal into the wok. At this point, it had been time for him to find some answers. After asking around, he learned that the girl had opened a pizza joint somewhere and was working there with an Italian American boy toy. I said to my friend, I bet the guy followed you from New York. That was when he turned on me and nearly hacked me into pieces with his meat cleaver.

I worked for two months at Kitchen X, but it felt like years. There were always endless amounts of dishes to be washed and trash to be taken out. In addition, there was the sadistic sous chef and the cold-blooded boss, Whip Cracker Zhou, next to whom it was always hard to resist muttering an obloquy. Even with only two shifts a week, the days felt like years. It's hard to imagine what it must have been like for Boss Li to spend all day in that restaurant that was once his. He grew feeble before he grew old, his hands and feet moved sluggishly; Whip Cracker Zhou said keeping him there was philanthropy, so of course, the wages did not amount to much. As such, my best friend always came to me to chat. After work, the two of us waited for the bus together. It was the middle of the night. Waiting for the bus could take an hour or two. He swore that that Italian woman loved him, at least at first, only later had she changed. The woman had said she was going to leave him, but that she didn't want his money. In addition, she had found him a wife, a Peruvian. The woman wasn't quite Black, nor white or anything, because South Americans are often of very mixed descent. He couldn't understand Spanish, she couldn't understand Chinese, and the lingua franca of America, English, was a language that neither of them spoke. Still, you could do it even without talking, so they did it, and babies popped out in twos and threes. They were not quite black and not quite yellow, taking on all sorts of shapes and sizes. Another strange thing was that the kids only listened to their mother, they couldn't speak a word of Chinese. When he came home, he descended into a speechless abyss. The place was creepy. Only by beating a few of the brats to tears could he feel a little release. He said to me, when he saw the houseful of little brats, he couldn't figure out what he had done with his life.

My friend told me that after introducing him to his wife, the Italian woman indeed had left his restaurant without taking a cent. What followed wasn't hard to guess. Sometime later, all sorts of people came with legal documents that he had signed. Under the name of Boss Li of Kitchen X, the woman had taken out several loans. Even selling the restaurant could not have repaid them all. There was his signature on those pages, but he had no idea what he had signed. At this point, he was still in love with her. He felt that losing his life's savings for love was at least a story. But one day, a thought struck him, and he brought a Chinese person who spoke Spanish over to ask his wife a couple of questions. Just as he had suspected, the Peruvian was a refugee without a green card. She had gotten it only after marrying him. By setting up this match, the adorable Italian had taken a hefty commission. Only then did he stop loving her.

Not long after I had left Kitchen X, Boss Li was fired by Whip Cracker Zhou. After that, he stayed home all day and drank himself into a stupor. He had grown old, and there were no more Chinese restaurants that would hire him. This story is rather a cliché, so I had never bothered to write it down. Suddenly writing about it now is because I have been trying to remember all my tales from America. The moral of the story is to remind you good fellows: if you want to get rich in America, first of all, it would be preferable to be a woman; second of all, go to Manhattan, don't go anywhere else.

The boss of Kitchen X in the abovementioned tale is named Whip Cracker Zhou. This brother had a face as long as a knife blade, clearly the cold-blooded type. He was too stingy to give his workers anything nice (and of course, too stingy to pay a decent wage), so everyone hated his guts. When some of those workers entered the kitchen, they grabbed any raw shrimp or fish they could find and ate it. They couldn't let Whip Cracker Zhou get all the advantages; as a result, their diarrhea was so bad that their faces shriveled. Apparently, someone even ate a whole chicken drumstick, even chewing the bone into a paste before swallowing it all. But I didn't see it, so I cannot confirm. One time, he went to New York for a few days. While away, someone used yellow paint to write huge characters on his wall "Whip Cracker Zhou." Eventually, the restaurant fell into disrepair and no longer looked like a business. I hadn't worked there for long before getting into an argument with Whip Cracker Zhou, so I went to work at a different restaurant. This other restaurant was a local fixture, with over ten years of history. The boss was around the same age as me, named Y. His restaurant was situated in a Jewish neighborhood. It was entirely unostentatious. He didn't advertise, so aside from neighborhood locals, not many people knew about the place. It was a building with dark, tinted windows. Other than the few Chinese words written on the wall, it didn't look at all like a Chinese restaurant. The employees of the place were diverse, including Chinese, Koreans, and even Roman-nosed Americans. Anyone who wanted to work there could do so. Once, there was a Korean girl, an artist with no shortage of money. When she learned that Boss Y was single, she forced herself to wash dishes there for a few months. But Boss Y pretended to be dumb and didn't take the bait. It made the girl so mad that she growled behind his back, pervert. After some time, when he still refused to take the bait, she stopped coming.

On the wall of Boss Y's restaurant, there hung a copy of the Heart Sutra written on rice paper. This is the most common of all sutras. It is included in its entirety in *Journey to the West*. When I was sixteen years old, I could already recite several parts of it: "*Gate! Gate! Paragate!*" When I saw the sutra, I didn't think much of it. I only thought the boss was funny for having written it all out. One day, an old Jewish man who had just moved into the neighborhood came in for a meal. After cooking up his food, Boss Y went out to chat with him. They had a lot in common, it seemed—they liked to make money and eat good food, and so on. Finally, he said, we all believe in a religion, only you believe in Judaism and I believe in Buddhism, that sutra there was written using my own blood. When the Jewish man heard this, he immediately stood up and stared at the sutra. He asked Boss Y to recite it for him. Before leaving, they shook hands and the man said: Boss Y, I have great respect for you, in a few days, I will bring some friends here. Only later did I learn that Boss Y really did use his own blood to write it, and it was blood cut from his own tongue. After writing out the sutra, he still had half a bowl of blood left, so he decided to write a few big calligraphy characters "proud to be born Chinese," and hung it next to the sutra. There was something irreverent about his attitude. In all seriousness, he would say to the foreigners: as a Chinese person, I am different from you all; but as a person, we are all the same, so you can trust me. Such can be considered a sort of business acumen.

This Boss Y was also a head chef, specializing in Sichuanese and Beijing cuisines. My ancestors were from Sichuan, Qu county and I grew up in Beijing, so as far as I could tell, his cooking was a bit Sichuanese and a bit from Beijing. Even so, some customers would say that the peppers in his kung pao were overcooked. Trying to cook authentically in America doesn't seem to come easily. From morning to night, he worked fifteen hours. As far as I know, he had gotten his American citizenship, but back in Taiwan, he was the son of a politician. Furthermore, he had an American master's degree in architecture, so he could have even gotten work as an architect. But frankly, if someone offered me as much money as he made, I would have taken it, but I wouldn't have wanted to do what he did—speaking of me, I was once a hard worker too. At sixteen years of age, I was sent to Yunnan to break new ground, sometimes working seventeen hours a day. But after all those years of hard work, I looked at the place before I left and saw that there weren't any new fields of crops, only a completely ruined landscape. After each rain came water and mud, no different from diarrhea. I became lazy after that. I went from working my heart out for no pay to never working unless I was broke—so I asked him about it. He said, running a restaurant was only right. With his business, he has helped many people, of course, including himself. There were indeed quite a few people working there at the time, even associate professors from top mainland universities. But the use of the word *help* sounded a bit contrived. Boss Y must have known about the theory of surplus value because when he asked me to talk about my previous experience at Kitchen X, he said: Xiaobo, tell us about how you were oppressed in the hands of Whip Cracker Zhou—he wouldn't use the word *exploited*. But at least his intentions were good. When he worked, he always tried to set a good example. When he finished cooking, he helped the sous chef take out the trash and helped me wash dishes, all while bellowing out a tune. At the time, most of the employees were from the mainland so guess what he sang—"Sailing the Sea Depends on the Helmsman." He even said: it's not a bad song, rather catchy. After closing time, when he would cook up a big staff meal of fish and shrimp, he would announce, "I am Boss Y, not Boss Zhou." That was how he buttered up his workers.

Putting aside how Boss Y saw himself, I want to mention a problem that all bosses share. Suppose there were no customers and the hostess at the front desk (overseas students) sat down somewhere to read a textbook, the boss would put on a surly face. In moments like those, the hostess should have been gazing longingly out at the street. That would have made him happy. That was his petty side. But he also had a generous side: once a year, he would rent a spot in the park and invite all his old customers and employees there for a barbecue. He also memorized the birth dates of many of his frequent customers and gave free meals to them on their birthdays. He was in the business of attracting returning guests. Each and every customer was an unforgettable part of his life—he also hoped that he and his restaurant could become an unforgettable part of their lives. This was his business plan. To execute it, he had to own respect and integrity.

Disclaimer: most of the content in this essay were stories I heard personally. I can guarantee the authenticity of every piece of information traveling from my ear to my pen. As for Yang Chuang-kwan losing his virgin powers along with his gold medal in Rome, I read that in a Chinese language newspaper in New York. I am clueless about sports so whatever people say is what I know.

WHY CHINA DOESN'T MAKE SCI-FI FILMS

ANG TONG ASKED ME a question, "Why doesn't China make sci-fi films?" To be honest, it would have been better to ask a movie director this question. I knew a couple of directors, so I asked one of them face to face. He let on a Mona Lisa smile that gave me goose bumps all over. After the smile, he yelled, "There's a lot we don't have yet! Don't give me that crap...." his bluster left me at a loss, unsure what kind of crap I was giving. Friends from the movie industry always have a nasty temper, I'm not sure why.

Since I couldn't get an answer, I tried to answer the question myself. When I was in America, I often went to the video rental store on weekends. There was a long shelf labeled sci-fi, but even though they were called that, most of them had nothing to do with science. For example, *Star Wars*, that's a modern-day fairy tale. Careful observers will notice the outlines of Snow White, Robinson Crusoe, as well as many other familiar characters. And as for *Jurassic Park*, that was more like a horror film. By sci-fi, they usually just mean that the story takes place in the future. Of course, to make these kinds of movies, some amount of scientific knowledge is indispensable. Of all the human endeavors, the one advancing at the most rapid speed is technology. Without some understanding of science, it would be hard to write anything convincing.

There is one American film called *The Fly*, which I believe many people in our country have seen. It's about a scientist whose research objective is to transport a human body via an electric cable. Unfortunately, when he tries to send himself, a fly gets into his machinery. After being transported, his genes are mixed with the genes of the fly. As a result, little by little, he mutates into a fly—after watching the movie, I felt nauseous because it had won the Oscar Award for best makeup that year. I believe the person who wrote this story must have been inspired by something Norbert Wiener once said, "In theory, it should be possible to send someone across an electric cable, but doing so would be too difficult, far beyond our current means." To find inspiration like that, you would have to know who Wiener was—he was the founder of cybernetics, once a child prodigy—I could go on, but where would I stop? In short, to make a movie like that, the director shouldn't go to a film academy, but a liberal arts school. You wouldn't even have to take science classes, just to listen when the science majors in your dorm room have random conversations. As far as I can tell, students in liberal arts schools enjoy having film students among them as well. Especially the guys majoring in science, they must want there to be girls studying performance art on campus . . . very necessary. Scientists have appeared from time to time on the Chinese silver screens, but none of them resemble the real thing. This is because film students never come across any scientists.

Movie actors tend to think that by the time a person acquires the title of a PhD, they've probably gone mad or at least cuckoo. That is far from reality. My wife is a PhD, if she acted like the people in the movies, I would have divorced her long ago.

Other than some scientific knowledge, making sci-fi films also requires imagination. As far as creators are concerned, this is the minimum standard. These movies take place in the future, so they are unconstrained by everyday reality. This offers the writer total freedom—it's also a very serious test. Once you enter the freedom of this imaginative space, if you can't make something interesting happen, then awkwardness will be inevitable. When you make historical films or films about ordinary life, even if you don't do a great job, at least it won't feel like a disgrace. The lack of scientific knowledge, the lack of imagination, these are the reasons why China can't make sci-fi films—but there's one more thing, to make a good sci-fi film, you need large sets, which require money—we are only in the early stages of socialism, still short on money. There, I've come up with a complete answer all by myself. But if I were to answer Wang Tong like this, I would still feel like something was missing . . .

When I asked a Chinese director friend why China hasn't made any sci-fi films, the guy got really angry. So let me put myself in his shoes: suppose I wanted to make a sci-fi film but lacked scientific knowledge, I could audit a university course. Suppose I lacked imagination, I could down a few shots and stare at a wall. An old saying goes, even cow dung left in the field will start fermenting and bubbling after a few days under the sun. If I drank two ounces every day and stared at the wall for three hours, year after year, I refuse to believe that I wouldn't have come up with something—even the best sci-fi scripts were thought up by humans, right? Eventually, I would have a script in hand and an investor willing to finance it, as for actors, they could go to a university research lab to experience that life, that's easy—at this point, I'm only left with one question: suppose the movie I wanted to make was *Jurassic Park*, how I would explain it to the government authorities? This movie of mine, where is the social value? Where is the moral value? Why do I want to make a weird movie like this? The most important question is: how is this movie contributing to the current national effort? I wouldn't be able to answer any of these questions, but that would be unacceptable. With this in mind, I finally have a decisive answer: I shouldn't have put myself through all this trouble in the first place.

MOVIES, CHIVES, OLD NEWSPAPERS

THE CHINESE MOVIE INDUSTRY, it seems, is reinvigorating its focus on propaganda and education. Those who work in the industry should be prepared for a period of hard work and sacrifice—it is our nation's glorious tradition. In the middle of the 1970s, when I worked as a street mechanic in Beijing, I often went to the movies. I never paid for tickets, they were all handed out from above. Theoretically, it was the labor union that bought the tickets. But where did the labor union get this money? Our union dues were only five cents a month. In the end, the money came from the government. Strictly speaking, movies then had no box office value, the state paid for the entire movie industry. In the future, this might be the case again. People say that the government should not be overly generous, so those in the movie industry should not have high expectation. That's what it is.

When the state spends money to let everyone watch movies, it is for the purpose of propaganda and education. To be frank, I haven't watched many of them. In '74, and '75, I had nothing to do so I went a few times. By the time '77, '78 rolled around, I didn't go to the theater once. At the time, I was studying to get into college, every minute was precious. The other young workers didn't go either. Some were making furniture in preparation for married life. Some were still dating. In short, everyone was busy. Young people told their older colleagues to go, but most of the older colleagues in our factory were women and they said that the theatre was too dark, they couldn't do their knitting—even though there are some who can knit in the dark, our colleagues said: we haven't learned that skill yet. As a result, the tickets that were handed out in the morning ended up in the wastebasket in the afternoon. What I want to say is, for movies to achieve the purpose of propaganda and education, people need to watch them. This is a serious challenge. It's not only up to the directors and screenwriters to rack their brains over it, other people can contribute ideas too. Based on my personal experience, I have the following suggestion: if the labor union can rent the whole theatre, they could keep the lights on so the female workers can watch the movie while they knit, this would guarantee an audience.

Of course, propaganda and education through movies cannot only focus on city folks, it also needs to reach the vast countryside. On this matter, I have some experience as well. In the early 1970s, I was stationed at a commune in Yunnan. There, a movie audience was never fussy. People would watch any and everything, even *News Digest*. But don't even think about box office numbers. There was an audience but no box office. It wasn't because people weren't willing to pay for tickets but because they didn't have any money there. I believe that showing movies in the countryside makes better use of the ability to propagandize and educate. By analogy, showing movies in the cities require box offices, making it like professional sport; showing movies in the countryside is more like amateur sport. Amateur sport is more in line with the Olympic spirit. But this line of work still requires professionalism, and a spirit of self-sacrifice—which is why I want to remind those who work in the movie industry to be prepared for hard work and sacrifice. This is especially true of the projectionists. When I was stationed at the commune, I got to know a few projectionists, so I have personal knowledge of the matter. At the time, I oversaw driving the oxcart. Every two weeks or so during the dry season, I had to pick up a projectionist, so I got to know them well . . .

Once, a projectionist with a big heart and a wide girth came to our team. He was easy to talk to, but unfortunately, I have forgotten his name. I not only picked him up but also picked up his equipment. Among his equipment was not only a projector but also a gas-powered generator. This way, he wouldn't have to use bicycle pedals to generate electricity. On our way back on the oxcart, I explained how envious I was of his position: think about it, he didn't have to stand down in the fields in the sun and wind. He had a machine to play with and didn't even need to use his legs to power it. But he told me that I was making light of the situation, and that the responsibilities of a projectionist were great. For example, when the feature is projected onto the silver screen, if for some reason, a giant head came out upside down, the crowd could be scared stiff. And suppose the face that was shown was that of the great leader, then there would have been no choice but get on his knees and slap his own face left and right while asking for the revolutionary crowd's forgiveness. If he was forgiven, then all would be well, but if not, he would have been publicly ridiculed and put in detention—these things happened, and they happened often. For some reason, the more the projectionists feared such calamities, the more they happened. According to him, projecting movies was even worse than working the field. But those were special circumstances during a special period of history, so there is no need to generalize. But he also added: propaganda is not an easy gig—a sentiment that is universal. Just take movies as an example. If you showed a commercial film and it tanked, it's because of your lack of professionalism; but if the movie had political motivations and tanked, in addition to being called unprofessional, you would also be seen as a political problem. Projecting films is like this, and producing films is even more so. It's a straightforward problem, so I won't dwell on it any longer.

The more challenging the job, the more it needs to be done, that's the spirit you'll need. The projectionist I picked up was precisely the type. When he showed movies to us, he didn't even get a wage, much less any kickbacks. The only thing we could offer were free meals, he could eat at our canteen. It all sounds very highminded, but it wasn't really. The place we lived in was a state-run factory farm and he was stationed in the rural film team. We all functioned within the same system, so there was really no point acting like strangers. On our way, he asked if the food in our team was any good. That wasn't a bad question: even though we were a factory farm, we had no equipment, only our hands. We ate what we grew, no different from the peasants. At the time, our harvest was terrible, so I said to him honestly, the food sucks. We planted some peanuts that got wiped out from disease, so we hadn't had any cooking oil for the past year. He asked me if we had vegetables and I said we did. He said, that's good. Some teams had lost all their vegetables, left only with bean stews. He had already eaten several meals of bean stews and didn't have the appetite for more. Our team had a bad habit called cooking for the crowd. When a chief came to inspect, there would be a feast, and even when a veterinarian came to castrate a bull, there would be a fried egg. But when a projectionist came, there was nothing special. I'm not sure why that was.

The reason I'm telling this story is to emphasize how hard it is to work in the movie industry. Having no wages isn't hardship. Having no cooking oil isn't hardship. What constitutes hardship is something I'm about to get to. When we got to our base, I helped him unload his equipment before heading off to the kitchen—other than driving the oxcart, I also helped in the kitchen. The fare that day was the same as usual, a chive salad. Because we had no oil, the only way to prepare the dish was as a salad. When I got to the kitchen, all the food was ready, so I brought out the rice and vegetables. Since I had been familiar with the projectionist, I served him two big ladles of the chives, so that he could eat a little extra. Afterward, I was also responsible for wiping down the kitchen and cleaning up; just then the projectionist charged in with his right hand choking his own neck. His tongue hung halfway out of his mouth like a hanged ghost. Of course, he still had his left hand free. He used it to point at his bowl—mixed in with the chives is a shred of old newspaper. As far as I could see, there was nothing all that strange. He asked: had the chives been washed? I said they were probably washed but I couldn't guarantee how carefully. He then asked: does your team fertilize your vegetables with manure? I said: don't know what else we could use to fertilize . . . only then did it occur to me that the old newspaper probably belonged to the team. All the parts of old newspapers that didn't have the faces of important people were used for going to the bathroom. Most of the newspaper ended up in the manure pit—when I thought about it, I felt sick as well and skipped that meal of chives. But admirably, after a spell of dry heaving, the projectionist went on to show the movie. After that, whenever he came to show a movie at our team, he either packed his own food or stood outside the door and took in big gulps of air. There, he blabbed to himself: I'll be full after eating some northwestern wind—the fellow had a sense of humor. Here, I need to clarify that I wasn't the one in charge of washing the vegetables. Had it been me, I would have deserved no less than death. This was a story I had seen with my very own eyes. A comrade projectionist full of caution, found a piece of paper in his chives and later ate the northwestern wind; that's what hard work and sacrifice mean. In comparison, the managers of movie theatres today only want to show commercial films in pursuit of profit. They don't hold social needs and propaganda work close to heart. What a shame! On the other hand, how do you make yourself full by eating the wind? That's something I still have to figure out.

BEGINNING WITH THE INTERNET

MY COMPUTER IS NOT CONNECTED to the internet yet, but I have thought about connecting it. I hear that the internet is full of pornography as well as all sorts of reactionary content. These stories have me scared. Some time ago, people were suggesting that the internet needs to be restricted. I am in complete agreement. To be honest, how can you just let information travel freely? But suppose that I do know a thing or two about this subject, I would have to say: unless you cut if off with scissors, there is no way to restrict the thing. It's too fast, too supernatural. Modern society is exploding with information. It would be too hard to censor everything even if you tried. It would be easier just to ban it. If I were a businessman or worked in technology, not having the internet would be problematic. But why should I be worried about businessmen and engineers? On the information superhighway, oceans of information roil. But I'm only a simple scrivener. I'm fine not knowing any of it. In conclusion, cut the internet off and spare me the headache.

The internet is a tool for transporting information. There are also tools for processing information, which are the varieties of personal computers. Think about it, without a computer, you can't connect to the internet. But then again, hard drives and CD-ROMs can also be used to sell pornography. So only by banning the computer would you get to the root of the problem. But now I'm feeling a bit reluctant—about ten years ago, I bought my first personal computer. I am now on my fifth computer. Besides all the money I've spent, I've also put in a lot of effort. I wrote all the software I use myself. I use it to write and to carry out scientific research: calculations, statistical analysis—by the way, using computers to do statistics is bliss. Without a computer, doing statistics is a major pain. But the darn thing didn't learn to be good. Instead, it started selling pornography. Since it brought it on itself, there's not much anyone else can do to save it. But considering our past ten years of friendship, I will say a word or two on its behalf: early computers were harmless. Those gigantic things the sizes of HVAC systems clanged as they calculated and were unable to show any pornography. It's only the 486s and 586s that came later which are guilty: their hardware has advanced in leaps and bounds, they are now capable of doing good as well as evil, so ban them . . . but if you wanted to buy an older computer model, you may not be able to. Therefore, I propose we ask IBM to restart an old production line for us, one which produces early computers. When a foreigner hears talk like this, their eyes bulge out and they ask: are you guys crazy? The right response should be: we're not crazy, you're crazy—but at the same time, we should make sure that they don't send our trade representative to an asylum. Of course, if we do decide to ban all computers, I can deal with it. I can write with paper and pen and do calculations on an abacus. Those who don't know how to use an abacus can count Popsicle sticks—of course a floor full of Popsicle sticks might look ugly, but—thank heavens, I no longer do many statistics these days.

In addition to computers, television and movies are also disseminating unhealthy information. In this regard, my attitude has always been firm: I support strong regulation. First of all, foreign films aren't compatible with our national condition, they should all be banned. Second, people in our film and television industries are a mixed bag, much of what they produce is awful. . . . I'm a novelist with very little to do with film and television, interested only in a modest living. People like Wang Shuo, Feng Xiaogang, and their whole coterie of movie stars aren't nearly as educated as me. I can't stand the stuff they produce, yet they've all made fortunes. There should be stronger supervision—but on the other hand, reviewing every piece of information on the internet before it is published seems untenable: even watching a TV series in 120 episodes is hard to accomplish. It would be easier just to ban it all. During the decade of the Cultural Revolution, I only ever watched the eight model films and yet I survived, didn't I? I'm not like these young people who can't do without audio and light and electricity and images. I would be happy just to read a book. After all this talk, I almost forgot about pop music. That mongrel garbage should be the first to be banned. If the young people get bored, they can exercise and play sports, crafting not only their spirits but also their bodies . . .

But banning things all around, the ban will eventually reach me too. The contents of my novels are healthy but I can't guarantee that every single one of my sentences is healthy. Besides, by then I would be so scared that I wouldn't have the wherewithal to explain myself. If TV and movies can be banned, then why not novels? We love to read but there are still those who are illiterate. I'm sure they would be perfectly happy to ban books. Fine then, I won't write anymore, I'll go to the bus station and help people load luggage. I'm healthy and strong, I can be a mover. Not like those other authors who can't even pick up a bag . . .

I support the shrinking of life's possibilities if mine are not the ones getting shrunk. But if the shrinking gets out of hand, the result might very well be beyond my reckoning.

In *For Whom the Bell Tolls*, Hemingway wrote something to this effect: we are all one, misfortune onto one is misfortune onto all. Therefore, don't assume to whom the bell is tolling for—it's tolling for you. But this way of thinking is unfamiliar to me. I'm more interested in other people's misfortunes. More than fifty years ago, a German Protestant pastor said: "At the beginning, they arrested Communists, I didn't speak up because I wasn't a Communist; then they arrested Jews, I didn't speak up because I was an Aryan; after that they arrested Catholics, I didn't speak up because I'm a Protestant . . . finally, when they came for me, there was no one left to speak up for me." But as we all know, we don't live in Nazi Germany and I'm not a Protestant pastor. Therefore, I'm not interested in remembering those words.

VISITING THE HOME OF AN AMERICAN LEFTIST

LAST WEEKEND, WHEN Mr. Huang came for a visit, he asked me whose music I liked to listen to. I couldn't remember the names of any singers so I blurted out The Beatles. In truth, I only occasionally use their music to put some noise in my ears. Right now, I still have a couple of cassettes put out by these four old Brits, but not even a single CD. As such, I can't really be considered a fan of theirs. When I hear their songs, I am revisited by some old smoky memories: many years ago, when I first arrived in America, I once visited the home of an American leftist late at night. At the time, The Beatles were playing on his old cassette player. Come to think of it, it was rather embarrassing. I didn't even know the guy, but a friend of a friend gave me his address. We went there at one or two o'clock in the morning and it was a group of four of us. To be honest, it wasn't really a friendly visit so much as trying to save on hotel money—hotels in New York are incredibly expensive. Had he not been a leftist, he would never have let us in, and might have even called the police on us. But the host was happy to see us, and we chatted all night. We talked about Che Guevara, Leon Trotsky, and even Hao Ran's novel *The Golden Road*. The gentleman had an English edition of *The Golden Road* on his shelf. It was published in China, translated by a friend of a friend. I flipped through it and thought that the translation wasn't great. Our new friend talked about their tumultuous sixties and seventies: the anti-war movement, the sit-ins, the big protests and demonstrations, and even mentioned how he excited he felt when he first read in Mao's Little Red Book "to rebel is justified." When he spoke, his eyes lit up. We also had some similar experiences, but we don't like to talk about it. He was always trying to get us to tell stories about the Chinese Red Guards, but we didn't want to. In short, he left me with the impression of having seen an old friend; we were once as close as hands are to feet, but we no longer had anything to talk about—to me, his thoughts reeked of ultra-left adventurism. By his logic, there was no reason for me to learn anything from America. I should have gone home to keep rebelling. I didn't think that was a good idea. But no matter what, American leftist are genuinely some of the nicest people, even right-wingers can't deny that.

I remember that this leftist friend had a head of long hair, wore a pair of slick oily jeans, and grew a big beard in which there were quite a few white strands. Inside of his tiny messy apartment, there was a middle-aged woman, who wasn't his wife. There was also a silly golden-haired girl, who wasn't his daughter. Overall, he didn't seem like a very successful person. But history will leave a note for his kind because they stood up and spoke out against the Vietnam War, against racism, and against all sorts of injustices. By dawn, we were all exhausted, but he was still in a talkative mood—it seemed he had been used to all-nighters. In the warring days of the sixties and seventies, they often camped out in the park, played guitar, and sang songs around a bonfire all night; they also smoked marijuana. This kind of life I've lived as well, except it wasn't in a park but on some hill. We might have been building a dam or logging on a hillside. A bunch of intellectual youths sat around a fire and sang all night. As for marijuana, I've never smoked any. Only once, when I ran out of tobacco, I rolled something out of these big tea leaves from Yunnan that was as thick as a chicken drumstick. When I lit it, a big puff of flames nearly burned off all my eyelashes. There wasn't any nicotine in the tea leaves but there was quite a bit of caffeine. After taking a puff, I felt like I had taken two bullets to my temples and immediately collapsed on the ground. Sadly, these experiences of ours had no real meaning, only some self-inflicted trauma. But I have nothing to complain about, only the sense that enough is enough, I want to try something else—that's the biggest difference between my leftist friend and me. But no matter what, of all the different types of Americans, I still like the leftists the best.

MY APPROACH TO REEDUCATING THE YOUTH

I HAVE A NEPHEW, SMART as a whip. Even though he didn't work hard in school, he still got into Tsinghua University—this fact can best be explained by his bloodline on his mother's side. As one of his uncles, I'm also hyperintelligent. The kid liked rock music. He went to class during the day and played guitar and sang songs at night. He even gathered up a few buddies. What they called "rehearsal," their neighbors called misery; the main reason for this is this noisemaking contraption connected to his guitar that could make the sound of a shattering iron wok. As for the homework Tsinghua University gave out, it was nothing to play around with. Whenever exams approached, he had to pull all-nighters and cram; as a result, he didn't have time to sleep. After a couple of semesters, his face became shriveled like a monkey, there were dark rings around his eyes, and his body was skinny enough to float. His plan was to make rock 'n' roll his career after he graduated. Not only did his parents feel a sense of impending doom, even I didn't think playing rock 'n' roll was a sustainable way of life—unless he somehow learned how to eat air and shit smoke.

As a rock 'n' roll-obsessed youth, my nephew might be able to find some opportunities to play weekends at a few bars, but he wouldn't make any money; suppose he annoyed the bar's neighbors, or got caught up in some sort of a "crackdown," he was liable to receive an invitation to the police station—I've heard stories like that. You often find these youths squatting in a line outside the police station as if they were in a public toilet, casually talking shit to the police comrades. Of course, in the end, they needed their parents to come and pick them up. This kid's parents are my older sister and brother-in-law. These types of situations are deeply troubling to them. They are what you would call "polite society," so you know they can't be losing face. The parents were always reprimanding him, but he wouldn't listen. The worst part about it was the fact that I was one of his role models. I've never stayed in a police station. I'm only a freelance writer. But for some reason, he felt that there were similarities between my job and rock 'n' roll. He would say with confidence: my uncle can understand me! Because of this, whether I wanted to or not, I had to take up the responsibility to persuade my nephew to not become a rock musician and instead focus on his field of study and become an appliance engineer. Even though this was all within the family, it could still be considered a form of reeducation. In theory, I should have started with ideals and morals but because it was between uncle and nephew, I cut straight to the chase: "Boy, your dad and your mom went through a lot to raise you. Why don't you just focus on school, find a decent job, and stop making them worry about you." His reply was of course, "That's what he wanted as well, but he couldn't do it." He loved his music too much. I said, "It's good to have hobbies.

But why don't you make some money to support yourself first, then work on your hobby? I don't know much about this rock 'n' roll music but I have heard the song 'Penniless.' The tune is catchy but simply judging by the title, it doesn't sound like a very happy life." My nephew immediately responded, "Uncle, what is the purpose of happiness? Suffering is the wellspring of inspiration. Didn't our forebears say: without suffering, how can you be called a poet?" I remembered that line from one of Lermontov's poems. If he knew that, then the situation was more dire than I had anticipated . . .

Suffering is the wellspring of artistic creation, there's no arguing with that: on stage, people sang "On the Loess Plateau" and "Penniless" on the silver screens, what you saw was *Old Well, Ju Dou*, and *The Story of Qiu Ju*. And it's not just in China, but overseas, it's the same way. Take music for example, Tchaikovsky's "Andante Cantabile" is a perennial classic. Supposedly, it was based on a Russian folk song "Little Ivan," another song of the suffering masses. Even American pop star Mariah Carey sings in the style of Black soul music, that's the music of Black African slaves . . . from this perspective, for my nephew to choose a life of misery in order to purify his soul and ascend to the peak of artistry was, in theory, correct. But I just had to tell him that it was wrong because he is my nephew and I had to answer to my sister. So what I said was: true, suffering is the wellspring of art; but it doesn't have to be your suffering . . .

Tchaikovsky wasn't Little Ivan; Mariah Carey never picked cotton in a Southern plantation; the people who sang "On the Loess Plateau" were all decked out in jewels; the actress who played Qiu Ju didn't look the slightest bit miserable once she sheds her makeup. She has plenty of money . . . and I hear she wants to marry a tycoon. All these examples point to a single truth: it is other people's suffering that is the wellspring of your art; if you went and suffered, then you would only become the wellspring of someone else's art. Because my nephew is bright, he got it right away. If his suffering became a wellspring of inspiration for someone other than himself, that would have been a bad deal—even though I don't really believe this, it was enough to convince my nephew. He agreed to focus on his studies and give up rock 'n' roll after he graduated. He would go into a corporation and make big money. After such a massive success, I felt like I was floating on clouds for days, as if I had learned a new trick. If there were other families with unruly children, they could hand them over to me for a little persuasion. I could even charge a fee and start up a second career in addition to my writing gig—a professional reeducator. The point of this essay isn't to brag about my newfound ability or to advertise my service. What I want to say is that there is more than one way to reeducate someone. This essay shows a sample of one strategy: by combining persuasion with dark humor, you open up a whole new world of possibilities . . .

WHY I WRITE

SOMEONE ASKED A MOUNTAINEER why he hiked—everyone knows how dangerous it is and there are no practical benefits. He answered, "Because the mountain peak is right there." I like this answer because it possesses a sense of humor—obviously he just wanted to hike but he had to make it seem as if it was the mountain that was making his heart itch. In addition, I like the mountaineer's pursuit, pointlessly climbing up cliffs. Hiking not only leaves you with sore muscles, but also puts you in danger of cracking your skull, which is why most people try to avoid hiking. From the perspective of thermodynamics, such a phenomenon exemplifies negative entropy. Anything that pursues disadvantage and avoids advantage is negentropic.

To say that writing is like mountaineering might sound contradictory right now. This is because in the past ten years, China has experienced a literature fever, a poetry fever, and a culture fever. Whatever the nature of the fever, the result is many people throwing themselves into writing. Some people think of me as just one of these people and caution me by saying, don't you know what year it is, why are you still writing novels (implying that we should now be having business fever, I should jump into the sea of commerce)? But my situation is different. For the first three fevers, I was studying in America, where I was not the least bit affected by the contagion. Our family creed dictates that children should not study humanities; science and technology are the only options. For that reason, the determination to write for me was exclusively a process of negative entropy. Even now, I can't understand why I do what I do, other than the fact that it is negentropic.

To say that my determination to write is a negentropic process requires further elaboration. Writing is an all-encompassing term, it does not matter what exactly one writes. Writing popular novels or romance novels should fall under the category of entropic behavior. The things I write aren't at all popular. Not only do I not make money, but sometimes I even lose some. The word *serious* in serious writers should be understood as such. As far as I can tell, most of the serious writers in this world don't truly qualify. With that said, everyone should now be able to see why what I do is truly negentropic.

The reason my parents didn't let us study humanities should be obvious. In the milieu in which I grew up, Lao She drowned himself in Taiping Lake, Hu Feng was jailed, Wang Shiwei was executed. Before that, there was Jin Shengtan's beheading and other similar examples. Of course, my old man was a pot calling the kettle black. He was a humanities professor himself but he explained that his choice had been a mistake and should not be seen as an example. The five of us brothers and sisters all ended up studying science and technology, except for my older brother. Considering my parents' foul tempers and thundering voices, you must admit that such a choice was negentropic. The exception of my older brother came about like this: in '78 when he took the college entrance exam, my older brother was the strongest miner of the Muchengjian coal mine in Beijing, his voice being even louder than my father's. In terms of beating him or yelling at him, even my father felt reluctant, so he had no choice but to let him study philosophy: he studied under the great lodestar of the logic world, Mr. Shen Youding. Considering how symbolic logic is a highly specialized field (from the point of view of laymen who don't read logic papers), it really isn't very different from science and technology. From the above description, you should begin to understand my father's intentions. He wanted us each to choose a field that benefits society but is also something that ordinary people don't understand so that we could live peaceful lives. My father lived a difficult life. He loved us more than anything in the world so for him to want such an arrangement for us is only natural.

My own situation is like this: ever since I was little, I wasn't especially strong and my voice was not particularly loud, so basically, I knew my place. Even so, there was always a part of me that had the dangerous urge to write novels. When I was stationed at a commune, I met a terrible person (he was our leader, one of our country's few bad cadres), so I came up with a story about a person who, starting from his tailbone, inch by inch, became a donkey, and wrote it down to vent my heart's rage. Later, when I began to read more, I learned that Kafka had already written a similar story, which left me rather embarrassed. There was another story in which the female protagonist grew a pair of bat wings. Her hair was green, and she lived in the water. I have already burned all these works from before my twenties. To bring them up now is to explain where my dangerous urge came from. After that, I repressed my urge and after finishing my undergraduate studies, I went to study in America. After my older brother finished his master's degree, he went to study in America as well. When I was there, I started writing stories, and from then on, this dangerous urge could no longer be suppressed.

While I was in America, my father passed away. Thinking back on why he told us to study science and technology, his reasons seemed to function by an entirely different logic compared to what I had experienced in America. It reminded me of what Marshal Tukhachevsky of the Soviet Union had said to the great musician Shostakovich, "When I was young, I was a musical prodigy. Unfortunately, my father couldn't afford to buy me a violin! If I had a violin, I would be sitting there in your orchestra pit."[23] The meaning of these words is not immediately obvious, so let me explain: this conversation happened in the 1930s in the Soviet Union. Not long after he said those words, the marshal breathed his last breath. In those years, they often executed marshals but not violinists. Those who jumped off buildings or hung themselves during the Cultural Revolution were predominantly the literary types. When my father was alive, he did all he could to provide us all with a violin, real or figurative: This violin could be any one of the STEM fields, and excluded only the humanities. This was completely different from what I had experienced in America, but the takeaway turned out to be the same—I should do something else; I shouldn't write novels.

As for America, everything can be summed up with the phrase: the business of America is business. This phrase implies that America is forever in the thralls of a business fever, always at a white-hot one thousand degrees. So if you had gotten the impression from what I have said so far that there was some sort of atmosphere

---

23. Paraphrase of Marshal Tukhachevsky's words, from Shostakovich's memoir *Testimony: The Memoirs of Dmitri Shostakovich*. Harper, 1979, 97: "How I wanted to learn the violin as a child! Father didn't buy me a violin. He never had the money. I would have been better off as a violinist."

there that encouraged writing, you would be mistaken. Even my older brother later regretted studying logic. He should have studied business administration or computer science. Even though he has yet to come up with a new logical theorem, when he sees rich people with their mansion, he can't help but complain about having shirked responsibilities toward his wife and kids.

In America, there is powerful force pushing people toward making money. Take housing for example, some people have a small lawn, some people a few hundred acres, and others have thousands of acres. Just in terms of housing, there are infinite reasons to want to make more money. Also take cars for example, there are countless models at a wide range of prices. If you have a lot of money, you could consider riding in the car in which Kennedy was assassinated. There are even people who buy old Soviet MiGs to fly around in. In their society, no one can stand their kids saying to their friends: my daddy is poor. If I had kids, I would be out there trying to make money as well. But writing books isn't a moneymaking profession there. If you don't believe me, just look at an American bookstore. All sorts of books crowd the shelves, as many as there are rows of toilet paper in the supermarket—if people are pouring their hearts and souls out onto rolls and rolls of toilet paper, it can't be a good business. Furthermore, there are many people whose books don't even make it onto the shelves and pile up in their homes. I don't have any kids and don't plan on having any. As a Chinese, I am a rare specimen. But every person has a face just as every tree has a bark. When other people are making money but you are off doing some suspicious work, it's hard to have much of a face.

In America, I once had a conversation with a Chinese American professor. He said that his daughter really showed promise. Instead of taking on a full scholarship to study anthropology at Harvard, she decided to pay her own way through an ordinary law school. To dare to go against the grain exemplifies her intellectual pedigree. But in fact, she only traded in a small advantage for a big advantage, accepted a small disadvantage to avoid a bigger disadvantage. If you don't believe me, just go and ask how much money lawyers make and how much anthropologists make. The professor I chatted with was a famous scholar, a man who went his own way. But when it came to his sons and daughters, he was no longer so eccentric.

After talking about America and the Soviet Union, it's time to talk about myself. At this point, I have been writing novels for eight years and published a few, but not many people have read them. Furthermore, I often receive contemptuous rejection letters. I try to stay positive and imagine: the person who wrote this letter must have gotten a scolding from his boss, so he's taking it out on me.

If you mention Wang Xiaobo, most people will think of the Sichuanese staff-wielding bandit from the Song dynasty, and not me. I am still in the process of negentropy. As an aside, human existence, civilization, and development are all negentropic processes, but here I'm talking about humanity. When it comes to me as an individual, I still can't explain what I'm doing.

As another aside, in terms of people in the process of negentropy, I am hardly the only one. In America, I met someone who set up a street side book stand selling works by Trotsky, Che Guevara, Chairman Mao, and so on. When I tried to talk to the guy, he first asked me if I was afraid of the FBI—and there are many more examples like him.

When you look at these people, you don't get a macroscopic view of water flowing downstream, apples falling to the ground, and wolves eating rabbits. Instead, what you see is water flowing up the mountain, apples flying into the air, and rabbits eating wolves. I should also add that a world with only entropy wouldn't work. Suppose everyone flowed naturally downstream, they would all end up together in the same depression, like maggots swarming in a manure pit. But this still cannot explain my behavior. It cannot be explained so long as you take the law of entropy as the preordained truth.

Of course, if I had to directly answer the question of why I write, I would say: I believe in my literary talent so I should do it. But this answer is about as believable as a murder suspect saying he didn't do it. It's up to you whether or not to believe what I say.

USING *GOLDEN AGE* TO TALK ABOUT THE ART OF FICTION

THE BOOK *GOLDEN AGE* includes five medium-length stories.[24] Of these, the story entitled "Golden Age" was begun when I was twenty years old and was not completed until I was nearly forty. Within that time, it went through many revisions. When reading my old drafts now, just about every sentence leaves me in a cold sweat. Only the last draft doesn't have that effect. In this thirty-thousand-character story, there are obviously still imperfections, but I no longer feel the urge to edit them out. This shows that it's possible to write a story in this way. Even though it's difficult, it's not impossible. This kind of writing is an

---

24. In 2022, Astra House published an edition of *Golden Age* that contained three of the stories—"Golden Age"; "At Thirty, A Man"; and "Years as Water Flow."

author's pursuit of perfection. I believe that each author has a particular sense of perfection, but that this perfection cannot be pursued every time. It was said that Friedrich Dürrenmatt also wrote *The Judge and His Hangman* over many years. Upon its completion, he said: I can never write a novel like this again. This means he also wrote like that. A person cannot make every piece of work perfect, but of course, perfection would be best.

Once, a girl asked me how to write a story, adding that she was thinking about writing something. I explained to her my process of writing *Golden Age*. The next time I saw her, I asked how her writing was coming along. She said, after hearing about how hard it was to write, she gave up on the idea. Actually, in this book, most of the chapters didn't have to go through such an arduous process of revision. But I do encourage all writers to give it a try. It's good for you.

Many parts of the book touch upon sex. This kind of writing can lend itself to controversy, inviting accusations of bawdiness. I don't know why the writing came out like that. Thinking back on it, it wasn't written for the sake of controversy or bawdiness but as the reflection of an age. As we all know, the sixties and seventies in China were an asexual age. Only in an asexual age does sex become an interesting topic. It's just like how during famines, eating becomes an important topic. The ancients have a saying: hunger and lust are natural. Wanting to love and to eat is an essential part of human nature. Their deprivation becomes an obstacle to human existence.

Of course, these obstacles are not the main themes of my story. The main theme is still a reflection on the human condition. The pivotal logic is that our lives are so full of obstacles—how damned interesting! This kind of logic is called black humor. I think black humor is my aura, I was born with it. The characters in my stories are always laughing, never crying. I think it's more interesting this way. The people who like my stories often talk about how they laughed from beginning to end and found them very interesting, etcetera. This shows that my works have their own readership. Of course, some authors believe that crying is more moving. The characters under their pens never laugh, only cry. That's also a way to write. They also have their own readership. A friend once said that none of my stories have ever moved her. She's the crying type. She read my story by mistake and felt disappointed. I want to explain this because I don't want anyone else to read my stories by mistake and feel disappointed.

Readers of serious literature are fewer and fewer, but their aptitude has greatly increased. In modern society, literature has become like opera, a form of high art. Literature has lost a portion of its readers—for example, those looking for moral guidance, those looking for political intrigue, those feeling sexually frustrated, those looking for some thrill, those with nothing to do and time to kill; only those who are interested in reading serious fiction are left. Literature has also lost many of its authors—some have jumped into the sea of commerce, others have turned to writing TV and movie scripts, the only ones left are those interested in writing serious fiction. I think this is a good thing.

ON WRITING STYLE

EVER SINCE I STARTED WRITING, I have wanted to talk to people about literary styles and voices, but I can never seem to find anyone to talk to. When I talked to nonwriters, they found the topic too dry; when I talked to writers, we could never really speak openly. If something is written, it will possess a style, a voice. You can't always talk about other people's voices and not your own. But to a writer, style is as sensitive a topic as sex is to an ordinary person.

Never mind what is fashionable. As far as literature is concerned, I think the best styles have been created by translators. Mr. Fu Lei's style is good. Mr. Ru Long's is even better. Mr. Zha Liangzheng's poetry, Mr. Wang Daoqian's prose . . .

Their styles serve as my lifelong models. I must admit that I have a special obsession with style and voice, and that other people may not feel the same way. But I believe other lovers of literature will agree with the following opinion: what makes a style effective are its rhythm and pace. Pieces that are written beautifully can bring me immense pleasure. Many years ago, when I was stationed at a commune in Yunnan, the local Dai girls had amazing bodies. When I saw them gently swaying in their tightly fitted tube skirts, I couldn't help but begin to follow. The pleasure of good writing can be compared to such a feeling. The whole reason why I started to write was because I was seduced by good writing—as for how well I write myself, that would have to be separate discussion.

Among the previous generation of writers, many wrote in either a regional dialect or in a way that hinted at the influence of a regional dialect. I call this the regional style. Works written in Hebei and Shanxi dialects were the most common. People from Hebei speak slowly, so their writing tends to drag. As for the Shanxi style, in my opinion it has an intelligibility problem—at least the term eggish (apparently, some areas in Shanxi refer to top cadres as "*eggish*") is not universal enough to be understood by most readers. Literary works published during the "cultural revolution" tended to use regional styles. At the time, writers felt that this made their writing seem more down to earth, closer to the workers, peasants, and soldiers, closer to the spirit of their revolution— therefore, regional styles can also be called revolutionary styles. But of course, not every regional dialect can be associated with the revolution. Only the regional dialects of the revolutionary heartland connote revolution. If you wrote in a Suzhou dialect, it would never sound revolutionary at all.

After the regional style, the most influential style would have to be Su Xiaokang's reportage style, otherwise referred to as the Xiaokang style. This sleek and superficial style has imitators even today. His style should be read with a nasal voice to achieve its full potency, and it works best with three-word phrases such as "the

People's Republic," "it was revealed," and such. In Xiaokang's writing, the former simply refers to the government and the latter simply refers to a message, both uses are malapropisms. If you write too much in the Xiaokang style, you will regress to illiteracy.

Nowadays, a new style seems to have emerged. We often hear Ma Xiaoqing and Ge You on TV talking about how something is "super" this and "super" that, which makes them seem super silly. They are illustrative of this new style, which we can call the sassy-bimbo style. Although writers of the sassy-bimbo style don't necessarily use the word *super* all the time, still, you get the sense that being a smart person feels super exhausting to them. At present, many female writers (especially the pretty ones) have started to use the sassy-bimbo style. They don't have to use the voice all the time, only a few sentences of it will make the author seem like a big dummy. I also feel that my life is super exhausting but I can't bring myself to write like them. After all, my intelligence is my livelihood. In theory, a silly writing style should be unpleasant to the reader, but then you look at the book covers and see the authors: they look pretty, their seductive poses appear to be directed at me. But even if their pictures are pretty, the real person behind them might not actually be pretty; even if their faces were covered in acne scars, they could have covered it up with makeup before taking the photo. In any case, I read some of their books—and after reading, I regretted it. Quickly forget all that silly talk before it influences you. Writers are afraid of bad writing precisely because they don't want to fall under its bad influence.

The popularity of the abovementioned three styles emerged because of the era's fashion sense. The popularity of the regional style came about as a result of people's desire to be more like old revolutionaries; the Xiaokang style became popular as a result of people's vapid posturing; as for the sassy-bimbo style, I think it came as a result of young women trying to make themselves appear more attractive. When a pretty girl puts on an air of silliness, she appears more adorable—that's how Ma Xiaoqing performs. The legendary beauty Xi Shi had angina,[25] which increased her cuteness, so there could also be an angina style. By extension, an even cuter style would be the "I need nitroglycerine now!" style. But at that point, we are no longer enticed. People know a thing or two about medical science these days. We know that angina can progress into myocardial infarction, and when a heart attack strikes, the patient may very well die. When the sassy beauty has a chance of turning into a stiff corpse at any moment, she is adorable no longer.

Like I said, style to an author is like sex to an ordinary person. Here, I should offer an illustration of how I feel about bad writing. Around the year 1970, in the middle of the summer, I passed by a city on the banks of the Huai River. At the time the city comprised only low, humble structures. It was hot during the day and even hotter at night. I couldn't fall asleep in my hotel room, so I went downstairs for a walk. There, I noticed a bunch of people chilling under a tree. It was strange: the local men still had their shirts on, but the old ladies were all practically naked. As a result, under the light of the mercury streetlamp, I was confronted with a horrifying sight. At the time, I thought: if I only I were born without a penis, perhaps I wouldn't feel quite as awful. That's how I feel about bad writing: if only I were illiterate, perhaps I wouldn't feel quite as awful.

---

25. According to legends, Xi Shi was one of the renowned four beauties of ancient China. Her beauty was said to be so extreme that when she would lean over a pond, the fish would be so dazzled by her appearance that they would forget to swim, sinking.

ON THE LITERATURE OF REPRESSION

THERE IS SOMETHING EXTRAORDINARY about Zhang Ailing's novels, which is the depth of her understanding of the lives of women. In China, there is a type of old woman whose attitude toward young women is such that so long as the girl is not her own daughter, she wants the girl to suffer: the girl must do everything without a moment of rest, and after the work is done, the old woman will say it's not good enough; she will nag from morning to night. To use a harsh phrase—she will find fault in the wind and shadows, she will curse the mulberry tree to blame the pagoda tree. Young women nowadays wouldn't put up with this kind of life for even a day. But traditionally, all the women had to put up with it. And by the time the young bride has simmered into an old hag, she would in turn become as nasty as her old mother-in-law. Zhang Ailing has a thorough understanding of this kind of life. Her novels get to the heart of the matter. But to be perfectly honest, I don't like them. I've always felt that novels can talk about suffering and hopelessness, but they shouldn't leave the reader in a state of frustration. The reason is simple: if you weren't frustrated before reading the book, you'll be frustrated after, and if you were already frustrated, then you'd become even more frustrated. Frustration is one of the Chinese people's greatest plights. At some point, some people will simply stop feeling frustrated because they too will have become "simmered old hags."

In terms of tormenting others, it isn't just a women's issue but a men's issue as well; it isn't just a Chinese problem, but a world problem too. I once read a story about seafaring that touched upon the same topic. The tormentor wasn't a mother-in-law but a ship's captain. I think the story was written by Mark Twain: there was once a nasty old captain who made his sailors spend all day scrubbing the deck, wiping the windows, washing the mast. Sanitation is certainly a good thing, but scrubbing the deck twenty times a day seems a bit excessive. One day, the sailors reported that everything had been cleaned. The old man got onto the deck to inspect, only to find that there wasn't a speck of dust to be found, so he said: all right, why don't you clean the anchor then. Washing and cleaning all day left the sailors deeply frustrated, that's obvious, but there was also nothing they could do about it: surrounded by the vast ocean, even if they had wanted to quit, they would have had to wait until they reached harbor. Indeed, for a woman, living in the traditional Chinese family was just like being on a ship at sea, only that this ship will never reach harbor. If your frustration gets too much, your only choice is to jump into the sea. I'm not kidding, when it came to suicide, women in old times were experts. The conclusion to be drawn from such an analogy is this: these kinds of stories only happen in isolated settings where people are wasting their lives. These stories evoke a sense of claustrophobia.

The main point of this essay isn't to talk about Zhang Ailing or stories of seafaring, but about the mood of repression and oppression in novels. Whether it takes place in the family or on the sea, for the individual, it is about being trapped in a tiny cage; for humanity, it is an insignificant fragment of a nightmare. The bigger nightmare is the state of society, more precisely, it is one's cultural backdrop. Suppose that for a long time, society doesn't progress, lives don't improve, and no new ideas come to surface, this could be considered an intellectual's nightmare. This nightmarish state will be revealed in literature. This is precisely one of China's literary traditions. In China, people believe that nothing under heaven ever changes. When they feel frustrated in their lives, they begin to harbor a deep sense of nihilism. The best example of this literary genre is the pulp fiction of the Ming and Qing dynasties. Zhang Ailing's novels also showcase a similar mood: there is sadness but no rage; there is hopelessness but no hate; they read like something written from the deathbed. The first time I read Zhang Ailing, I was in America. I found her works rather strange. When I returned to China and read some of the works by young contemporary authors, I also had a similar feeling. Only then did I realize: maybe it was me who was strange.

The so-called literature of repression has the following characteristic: it writes about the cage and the nightmare as if they were everything. You are either a bride living in frustration, or you are a mother-in-law annoying others; you are either blaming yourself for all your frustrations or you're being nostalgic about what you once had. In short, it's always a competition over who is more miserable. I find it hard to agree with such a world view. I majored in science. Scientists believe that there is no jail that cannot be broken out of and no nightmare that will not give way to a woken life. The only misfortune in life is one's own lack of ability. For example, for a mathematician, if you can prove Fermat's last theorem, you will win the esteem of the world's mathematical community and experience indescribable joy. The only problem is you haven't done it yet. If you are a physicist and discovered cold fusion, you would feel instant gratification. But the problem is also that you haven't done it yet. So the only takeaway is that you have to try harder. Think as if your life depended on it, that's the only way to save yourself.

It is with such an attitude that I have thrown myself into my writing career. For me, there is more to writing than talking about the same old office drama and the same old interpersonal conflicts. One could, for example, write an *Alice in Wonderland*, or a work like Italo Calvino's *Our Ancestors*. Literature could be just like science, a boundless domain in which people can launch their tsunami-like imaginations. But of course, this could also be a terrible idea. I have personally written a series of such novels about everything under the sun other than seafaring and cages. Sadly, these books are still in the hands of the editors, unable to be published. These editors even have to pose the ontological question, "Where is this guy from? Who is he? What exactly is he writing about?"

CULTURE WARS

IN **BERTRAND RUSSELL'S** *Power: A New Social Analysis*, he mentions the concept of clerical power, which was once wielded by the clergy. He adds, in the West, intellectuals are the heirs of the clerical class. In addition, Russell states that in China, Confucian scholars also wield clerical power. That leads one to assume that in China, intellectuals are the heirs of Confucian scholars. Clerics and Confucians possess knowledge derived from sacred texts, the Holy Bible, the Analects, and such. Yet modern intellectuals, for the most part, do not carry around sacred texts. Their persuasiveness derives entirely from knowledge; a type of knowledge that is inherently persuasive. But the funny thing is the latter form of knowledge does not bring with it power.

Placing Confucianism side by side with religions will inevitably invite controversy. Confucianism does not adopt the name of God, nor does it use heaven and hell to scare people. But it too, relies on a mythology, which is that without it, people will have no ability to govern. Chaos will reign under heaven. Order, ethics, morality will all be gone. This mythology has intimidated generation after generation of Chinese people. Even now, some people believe it. Russell states that people's deference toward scholars never comes from an understanding of truth but from the magic that they imagine the experts possess. I believe that the magic of Confucianism is precisely the myth of governance. Of course, based on its content, Confucianism is a type of philosophy, but the words of the sages contain only conclusions and judgments, while they lack in evidence and logic. Without considering its myth about governance, its conclusions would not be very convincing.

When Russell talks about "truth," he is talking about science. This is a type of knowledge that can be acquired by anyone with normal mental capacities if they are willing to put in the work. As is well known, science cannot solve all problems, especially when it comes to value judgments. As such, some people consider it shallow. However, if you only spent some time studying it, you would find that it is very different from Confucianism.

We understand that the foundation of Confucian learning is memorization. One must remember every single sentence uttered by the sage. I believe that if Confucius and Meng-tzu came back to life and saw how their descendants continue to repeat their words, they would find it strange. Of course, not all students of Confucianism are merely record players. After all, they add their own phrase before the sage's words, namely, "Confucius says." Such an absurd phenomenon reveals the spirit of Confucian learning: to become copies of the sage. This copying process takes the form of memorization. On the other hand, one could also believe that these Confucian scholars have another motive. As we know, some people use the *Merriam-Webster's Dictionary* to study English. Compared to memorizing the books of the sage, memorizing the dictionary imparts almost no material advantage. Suppose you were able to become the sage's copy, then you would possess the magic of governance. You could show your meritocratic credentials and be elevated into officialdom; but memorizing the *Merriam-Webster Dictionary* will only qualify you to be a translator and earn you twenty yuan per a thousand words. These two exercises in memorization cannot even be mentioned in the same breath.

Now let us look at science. Its complexity aside, it is something that one agrees with as soon as one understands it. It is different from the idea that "rulers rule, administrators administrate, parents parent, kids kid" and different from "the unity of heaven and man." I've known these two sentences for many years and still don't agree with them. More importantly, science doesn't encourage scholars to become the clones of certain paradigms, nor does it claim to have some sort of magic. Because our Western intellectual counterparts brought up this idea, they no longer enjoy the deference they once did. If we believe what Mr. Russell is saying, Western intellectuals basically blew their own gig. Regrettably, they didn't only blow their own gig but they also blew the gigs of Chinese intellectuals too. Even more regrettably, there are some Chinese intellectuals who want to blow our own gigs as well—yours truly being one of them.

Ever since the beginning of modernity, people have been debating about the merits of traditional culture. We know that culture is the way people live, it is multifaceted. But the debates over tradition have always taken place at the level of philosophy, which is why the term *culture war* is not very fitting. In this debate, it is always mentioned that China's situation is unique. In my view, one side of the debate is always hinting at the magic of traditional governance, implying that China cannot be divorced from this magical force. If my understanding is correct, talking about divorcing China from this magical force actually involves two distinct issues.

One is whether the descendants of Confucian officialdom can be divorced from this magical force. The other is whether China's proletarian masses can be divorced from this magical force. To mix the two issues together is clearly inappropriate. Taken separately, the first question should be simple to answer. After having lost the myth of governance, the descendants of the Confucian officialdom, even if they find careers as professors and researchers, do not enjoy a status comparable to that of their ancestors. In relation to this phenomenon, Mr. Russell has something like the following to say: "When intellectuals found that their prestige has suffered as a result of their own activities, they began to feel resentment toward the modern world." There, he was talking about the situation in the West. In China, the sentence should be rephrased as: when Chinese intellectuals found that their prestige suffered because of the activities of Western intellectuals, they began to hate Western learning and foreigners in general. As for the second issue, the more you think about it, the harder it is to make the case. I have always suspected that people are thinking about the first issue while talking about the second. To be honest, I wish my suspicions were unwarranted.

We know that successful generals always pick their battles. For generals to be strategic is a good thing, but whether it is good for scholars to be strategic is another question. Those who support traditional culture have a theory that all tribes need to respect their own cultural tradition, or else there is no future for them. It is the opinion of yours truly that such a line of reasoning raises the suspicion of being overly strategic. On the battlefield of tradition, Confucians have more to gain than other people. Non-Confucians have every reason to avoid such a challenge. Not long ago, yours truly participated in a debate. In this debate, some men wanted to return to the traditional arrangement where men rule outside the home and women rule inside the home; several women participants disagreed. Clearly, on the battlefield of tradition, men have more to gain than women. Even though I am a man, I stood on the side of women; it was because I hate these underhanded tactics.

Now let us return to the main point. Mr. Russell once said that he supported the idea of universal equality. But unfortunately, reality is never quite like that. People are not equal, especially when it comes to their knowledge. With differential knowledge comes power. Suppose that everyone in the world was ignorant and there was only one person who was omniscient, that person would easily acquire power. Traditional Chinese sages thirsted for knowledge at least as much as modern scientists. As far as I know, the sage Zhu Xi had a lust for learning second to none in history. The difference between scientists and sages is that in addition to knowledge, scientists also want proof of that knowledge. Unfortunately, proofs can be understood by everyone. As a result, it no longer affords power. In comparison, sages were much cleverer. It was easy for them to achieve the status of omniscience, what we call the "inner sage"; unfortunately, such a title has very little to do with whether they can solve problems reliably. We know that inner sage and outer king are usually used together as a phrase. If we were to say that the reason why the inner sage has to be the smartest man in the room is for the benefit of the outer king, then we have committed the fallacy of assuming one's intentions. Fortunately, we have Zhu Xi's words to set us straight: he admits that his knowledge of all things is for the purpose of governing all under heaven.

Now, if I were to claim that Confucian ethics and moral philosophy is all wrong, I would have no evidence. I cannot even say that this body of knowledge is embarrassing. However, there is something embarrassing about this body of knowledge because certain followers have used it to usurp power. As for the inventors of this body of knowledge, by which I mean Confucius, Meng-tzu, not Zhu Xi, they are innocent. They did not acquire or enjoy any sort of power. If there are still people today attempting to revive this sort of knowledge to acquire power, we would have to use one of Mengtzu's sayings to criticize them: "There is nothing more shameful than being shameless." Of course, there will be those who say, I want to revive traditional studies to bring salvation to the people and to bolster their cultural self-esteem. In other words, they are morally superior and feel responsible for the world. All I can say to that is such a brazenly self-serving attitude is not my style; at the same time, I would fear that the clerical power is once again knocking on our door. Clerical power is clearly better than unfettered violence, that much I agree. Phoniness has always been preferable to violence. But then I think, living at the end of the twentieth century, shouldn't we hope for something a little better? Of course, one could respond to my hope by saying, isn't that too much to ask for as a Chinaman? —to which I can only cry to a wall with nothing more to say.

ITALO CALVINO AND THE NEXT MILLENNIUM

A **FRIEND SENT ME A BOOK,** Italo Calvino's *Six Memos for the Next Millennium*, which I am currently reading. The book comprises a series of lecture notes. But before having the chance to give the lectures or even finish the manuscript, the author died. The lecture notes are organized according to the following table of contents: Lightness, Quickness, Exactitude, Visibility, and Multiplicity. The last piece, "Consistency," was left unwritten; which is why I have been scratching my head all day wondering what he could have written, what is "consistency"? According to Calvino, literature will continue to flourish in the next one thousand years and these six lines of literary heritage will expand far and wide. I have always liked Calvino and after reading this book, I like him even more.

Calvino's *Our Ancestors* is beloved by all who read it. This was a work from his younger days. I think it fits under the rubric of lightness. In his middle age, he began to explore literature's infinite potentials. I have read a work representing this period, *Invisible Cities*—a book that isn't necessarily liked by all who read it. It would be too much to ask for everyone to like all his books, but I think you should at least appreciate his idea: literature has infinite potential. What could be wrong with that? Sometime ago, a friend read my works and commented: it seems like there are still new ways to write a novel—the remark left me in a sweat: I haven't even begun to explore the infinite and am still far from catching up with Calvino. I thought that my friend's point was problematic—had he not been a PhD in the literature department but rather an ordinary reader, it would not have been as alarming.

Mr. Editor asked me to write a little piece for a teahouse chat. I ended up talking about Calvino's literary heritage, not really a topic suitable for a cup of tea. To be honest, I don't know what I could chat about in a teahouse. I don't have cats or dogs, and I certainly don't own a car. When other people are playing with their cats and dogs, I am either tinkering with my computer or thinking about literature—if you want to listen to me talk about computers, I can say a thing or two. Right now, in Zhongguancun, you can get 8MB of memory for two hundred and fifty yuan, way too cheap ... but that is probably an even less suitable topic for the teahouse. Perhaps I will get a cat or a dog and buy a car, so that I can torment myself—by the way, the prices of cars are truly shameless. A low-end Korean model costs three hundred thousand and up, a price unheard of anywhere in the world. As for cats and dogs, I consider them meat. I have eaten one cat, five dogs, this was more than twenty years ago. From the perspective of cat and dog lovers, I am a cannibal. Therefore, I can only talk about Calvino ...

Calvino's *Invisible Cities* is a story that goes like this: Marco Polo stands before Genghis Khan, describing to him every city he came across on his journey east. Every city is a crystal clear symbol. After reading the book, I had a dream, each of the cities was like a strangely shaped sky lantern floating in nothingness. An ordinary reader would say, great, I see the city, now tell me the story of that city—but for Calvino's limitless mind, telling a story would not have been hard. However, he does not tell a single story, he just continues to describe new cities. Even until the very end of the book, he isn't done giving examples of cities. I get what Calvino was trying to do, more or less: an author wants to incorporate all the elements that make up a work of fiction: it should contain lightness, quickness, exactitude, visibility, multiplicity, and finally consistency. With all these elements at play, any story will turn out interesting and satisfactory to all readers. Unfortunately, this is easier said than done, but it must be tried—the reason is to ensure that we will not run out of books to read in the next millennium. I don't think this is a topic that very many people will find interesting—unfortunately, it's all I know.

THE SILENT MAJORITY

1

In *The Tin Drum*, Günter Grass wrote of a boy who didn't want to grow up. Young Oskar finds the world around him too absurd, and quietly resolves to always remain a child. Whereupon some otherworldly power fulfills his wish and he becomes a midget. This story is a little on the fantastical side, but very illuminating. Though it's impossible to always remain a child, it is possible to always remain silent. Many people around him have personalities much like mine—on public occasions we won't say a word, but we can hardly stop talking in private. Put another way, we will say anything to people we trust, and nothing to those we can't. At first I thought this was because we had lived through the cruelties of the

Cultural Revolution, but later I discovered this is common among all Chinese people. The writer Lung Yingtai,[26] exasperated, once asked why Chinese people never spoke. She had lived abroad for many years, and had more or less become a foreigner, frank and plainspoken. She viewed silence as a form of cowardice, but this is incorrect; silence is a lifestyle, one chosen not only by Chinese, but also by foreigners.

Here's one example I know of: Dmitri Shostakovich, a composer from the former Soviet Union. There was a long period of time during which he only wrote music, refusing to say a word. Later, he dictated a thick book of memoirs, signed his name on each page, and then died. As I understand it, the subject of his memoirs is for the most part his experience of keeping silent. I found great pleasure in reading the book—of course, I myself was in silence at the time. But I lent the book to a friend of mine who belonged to the circles of speech, and he gained no pleasure from it whatsoever. He found it dismal and depressing. One passage in the book described the Soviet Union in the 1930s, when people were abruptly disappearing, everyone was very frightened and no one spoke to one another. When neighbors had a dispute they didn't dare quarrel, and so expressed themselves by other means, which was to spit into each other's teakettles. I haven't a clue as to what Shostakovich looked like, but every time I imagine him doing this I burst out laughing. My friend did not laugh at all when he read this passage; he felt that spitting was ugly, low-class, and unenlightened. I hardly dared debate the point with him—further debate would have fallen under the purview of speech, and speech is the line of demarcation between the world of yin and yang.

Readers of *The Tin Drum* know that young Oskar changes his mind later, and grows up. I have chosen to speak now, meaning

---

26. Lung Yingtai is a very respected Taiwanese essayist and cultural critic who also served as Taiwan's first cultural bureau chief (1999–2003) and first minister of culture (2012–2014).

that I am no longer young Oskar, I am old Oskar. Now I agree, of course, that spitting in other peoples' teakettles is low-class and unenlightened, but certain similar things continue to happen around me. Here's an example familiar to any apartment dweller: if someone keeps leaving their bicycle outside your door, blocking your way, you don't have to keep silent. You can call the neighborhood residential committee, or talk to the bicycle owner directly: "Comrade, please recall the Five Lectures and Four Beauties."[27] As for the language he may use in return, I can make no guarantees. At the very least I expect he'll call you "nosy," and if you happen to be a woman he might call you a "nosy biddy," regardless of whether you're old enough to be a grandmother or not. Of course you can always choose the way of silence in expressing your displeasure, and let the air out of his tires. Just take care that he doesn't see you doing it. Or you can do something worse, which I won't recommend: stick a tack in his tire. Some people pull the tack out again afterward, making it very difficult for the bicycle owner to find and fix the leak. If the bicycle can be moved, then taking it someplace where the owner is unlikely to find it is also an option. I'll stop here, before I give anyone ideas. All this puts me in mind of what Foucault said, that discourse is power. That ought to be switched around: power means discourse. In terms of the above examples, if you're going to say "Five Lectures and Four Beauties" to someone, you'd better be wearing a red armband.[28] In my understanding even a red armband might not be enough: a police uniform would be better. Saying "Five Lectures and Four Beauties"

---

[27]. "The Five Lectures, Four Beauties, and Three Loves" are ideological education slogans promoted in China in the early 1980s. The Five Lectures refer to civilization, politeness, hygiene, order, and morality. The Four Beauties refer to mind, language, behavior, and environment. The Three Loves refer to love for the People's Republic of China, for socialism, and for the Communist Party of China.

[28]. A red armband is worn by the local citizens who are part of the neighborhood residential committee.

is a positive thing, naturally, but it's still safest to back it up with force or status. And now you see why, when my friend started talking about Shostakovich, and ugliness and enlightenment, I kept silent. He was a very good friend, but I was still afraid he might give me up.

Most people enter the classroom by the age of seven. I believe it was a little earlier for me, because as far back as I can remember there was a loudspeaker installed outside which kept up a racket throughout the daylight hours. From this speech I learned that one could smelt steel in an open earthen hearth. These resembled the ranges we used for cooking but with a small bellows attached, which would buzz and hum like a group of dung beetles in flight. They smelted cherry red flakes of metal, stuck together in blobs that looked like cow manure. That was steel, an uncle holding a drill rod told me. I was six, and for a long time afterward whenever I heard the word *steel*, I'd think of cow manure. From that speech I also learned that one mu[29] of land can produce three hundred jin[30] of grain; then we nearly starved to death. In short, ever since I was young I haven't had much faith in the spoken world, and the more vehement the voice, the more fervently it is pitched, the more I doubt. This habit of doubt had its origins in my starving belly. Compared with any speech, starvation holds the greater truth. I had another bad habit, in addition to doubting speech, and that was eating pencils. In elementary school, I'd start eating a pencil the moment I was seated at my desk. They were the kind of pencils with an eraser on the butt, one mao three fen each.[31] I'd start at the back and eat the soft delicious eraser first, then the pliable metal band. Past that, the wooden shaft was tasteless and

---

29. Mu is a Chinese unit of land measurement which can vary with location usually describing 666 square meters.
30. Jin is a Chinese unit of weight measurement corresponding to 500 grams.
31. The Chinese yuan is divided into mao and fen: ten mao are needed for one yuan, and ten fen for one mao.

unappealing, but it had a perfumed sort of scent that drove me to keep eating. Finally, there would be nothing left but the core of lead, which I'd wrap in a rubber band and continue to use. It wasn't just pencils: my textbooks, exercise books and even desktops were edible. Some I consumed altogether; others I left gnawed beyond recognition. There is a truth here, too, though one that has not been expressed in words: starvation can turn a child into a termite.

There is a great misconception in the world, which is that speech conveys people's ideas. If that were the case, then speech would be the perfect embodiment of thought. I say it's a misconception because there is always a hidden meaning to things, and speech can convey much which seems contradictory to what is said. Ever since I began to be aware of things I've heard people say: *Our generation was born in a sacred time; how blessed we are; to us is given the sacred mission of liberating all the world's suffering people*, and so forth. People of a certain age found this talk deeply inspiring, they loved to hear it. But I was always a little doubtful: how did I manage to stumble into so many wonderful things? Furthermore, I found this way of talking too unreserved. And reservation was a part of my upbringing. One day during the three years of trouble,[32] our family sat down to dinner and found a little piece of bacon in every bowl. When my younger brother saw this, he was unable to contain his elation, he ran to our balcony and shouted for all the world to hear: our family has meat for dinner! Then he was dragged back inside by my father and beaten savagely. This sort of education has left me rather withdrawn. So, listening to others talk about how blessed we are, how sacred our mission, how others are suffering but we do not suffer, I always think: supposing we really are as lucky as all that, wouldn't it be better to keep it to ourselves? Of course, I'm not saying I won't carry out my sacred duty. But here's

---

32. This refers to the Great Leap Forward (1958 to 1962), where in the last three years, millions of people starved to death.

what I think about all the world's suffering people: instead of constantly telling them how we're going to liberate them and punish their oppressors, wouldn't it be better to keep quiet, and then one day liberate them all of a sudden, and give them an unexpected treat? In short, I'm always considering the practical aspect of things, and considering them very carefully. Childhood experience, upbringing, and cautious nature have all led me to keep silent.

2

When I was young, speech seemed to me like a cold pool of water, it always gave me goose bumps. But no matter what, people come into this world as to the water's edge, and they've got to jump in sooner or later. I never imagined I would keep silent right up to the age of forty; if I had, I might not have had the courage to go on living. But at any rate, the speech I heard was not always that crazy—it was crazy and sane by turns. Before the age of fourteen, I hadn't yet resolved to live a life of silence.

When we were young, it was our place to listen to the speech of others. Later, when people of my age began themselves to speak, it made a terrible impression on me. A friend of mine wrote a book about her misfortunes during the Cultural Revolution, the book was titled *Blood Lineage*. As you can probably guess, her family background was considered problematic. She wanted me to write a preface to the book, which got me thinking about the things I had seen and heard during those years. When the Cultural Revolution began I was fourteen years old, in the first year of middle school. One day one part of our class suddenly belonged to the "Five Reds," while another part belonged to the "Five Blacks." My own situation was an exception; it wasn't clear to which group I belonged. Of course, this red and black business wasn't our own invention, and we hadn't initiated the change. In that sense we were not to blame. A few among us should be held responsible for bullying classmates, is all.

As I see it, the red students had all at once gained a great advantage, and thus deserved congratulation. Our black classmates were all at once saddled with great misfortune, and deserved sympathy. But before I could go around expression my congratulations or sympathy, some red students shaved their heads, strapped on big leather belts, and stood at the gate of the school asking everyone who entered: What's your background? They questioned their own classmates particularly closely, and when they heard tell of a background they did not approve of, they would hiss one word between clenched teeth: *Whelp*! Of course I could understand their delight at suddenly belonging to the Five Reds, but that they should therefore call their classmates whelps in public was surely going too far. I thought then what I think now: speech may have a great deal to teach us, but good and evil are nevertheless self-evident. What speech is forever teaching us is that we are born unequal. That some should be high and some low is an eternal truth, though you may choose to disregard it.

When I was in sixth grade, the reading given over the summer was *A Letter from the South*. It was about the Vietnamese people's struggle to resist the United States and save their country, and it was full of executions, beatings, and torture. Reading it filled me with the strangest ideas. I was entering puberty then, more or less on the verge of sexual deviance. What I'm saying is this: suppose that education had had its full intended effect; suppose those "tenders of the human garden," those "engineers of the human soul," had realized their designs for me; how could I possibly have escaped with my humanity, and resisted becoming bloodthirsty and cruel? Fortunately, people do not learn only from books, they also learn from silence, and this is the chief reason for the survival of my humanity. As for speech, what is taught me was: all "bull-demons" and "snake-spirits" must be swept aside, the Cultural Revolution must be carried out to the bitter end. During that time, speech stood in direct opposition to humanity. To believe it entirely would be to relinquish one's humanity.

3

I'll explain how my humanity survived intact: At the very beginning of the Cultural Revolution, I was living on a university campus. One day, returning from outside the campus, I met a large crowd entering by the front gate, their voices pitched high; of course they debated in the popular argot of the day, and in addition to Chairman Mao's teachings, they kept bringing up the "Six Points." These were rules that the central government had issued regarding the progression of the Cultural Revolution, one of which was "Conduct Verbal Struggle, Not Armed Struggle": a rule simply made to be broken. One person stood at the center of this quarrelling group, but his lips were tightly sealed, he didn't say a word, and there appeared to be blood at the corner of his mouth. Half the students present were pressing him with questions and urging him to speak, the other half were protecting him, telling him to keep silent. This was unusual. As for the rest of the trailing crowd, they were mostly boys of about my age, their lips tightly closed, not saying a word, no blood on their mouths, following behind like damned souls. Some of the college students wanted to hold them back but couldn't—when they blocked the way forward the boys just went around them, keeping silent throughout. This was a strange sight indeed, because the boys from our compound were typically ferocious. They thought nothing of quarreling or fighting, and even college students might not have been a match for them, but today they were surprisingly docile. I immediately joined them and asked what was happening but, strangely, the boys ignored me. Their mouths tightly closed and their eyes straight ahead, they marched forward steadfastly—as if they were all in the grip of some mass hysteria.

As we understand mass hysteria, there's one type where the subjects do not speak, only flail and dance about. Another type results in unceasing chatter, without the flailing. All that the two types have in common is a complete disconnect between that which is thought and that which is expressed. In the northern village in Yunnan where I was a sent-down youth, there was mass hysteria among some of the women, one of whom—if you were inclined to believe her—was the spirit of a fox that had died many years ago. She constantly argued and fought with her husband (who—again if you accepted the premise—was a beast), and demanding that, as a fox, she should be fed meat. When presented with a chunk of flesh, however, she demanded that it be cooked and served with garlic. Obviously, this was ill-suited to a fox's diet, and in fact it was she, not it, that wanted to eat meat. The Cultural Revolution, on the other hand, did seem a bit like mass hysteria, in that what people were thinking was not what they were shouting out loud. Of course, this interpretation takes into account the world of the yin. If you only consider the world of the yang, the conclusion must be that all that violence and chaos really was to protect Chairman Mao, and to protect the Party core.

But the boys from the college campus were not hysterical. I grabbed one I knew well and got the whole story out of him: Two students had met that morning, and started arguing about their differing points of view. The argument went on, and eventually turned into a fight. One of them was hurt, and sent to hospital. The other wasn't hurt, and so was naturally blamed as the aggressor; this was the boy now walking at the head of the group. In theory, the crowd was on its way to some organization or other (either the Campus Revolution Committee or the Preparations Committee, I can't remember which) to state their case but in truth they were just engaged in aimless Brownian motion[33] around the campus. There was another piece to the story: The wounded student had been beaten shapeless, and a part of his ear could not be located. Some Agatha Christie-style reasoning determined that the piece of ear could only be in the mouth of the student who had administered the beating, providing he hadn't swallowed it. This particular gentleman not only had a violent temper, but could bite repeatedly. Anyway, he now had two choices: either spit the ear out in front of everyone, proving his dastardliness, or swallow it. When I heard all of this I instantly joined the following crowd, pressing my lips together, clamping my jaw shut, even feeling I held something slightly salty in my mouth.

Now I must admit I didn't see the conclusion of this business; the day was getting on, and there would have been trouble if I'd returned home late. But I was very wrapped up in the outcome of events; I hardly slept that night. Someone else told me how it ended: the biter finally spat out the ear, and was then apprehended. I don't know what you'll make of this story, but at the time I felt as if I'd been relieved of a great weight: humanity had ultimately prevailed. Humans will not eat their own kind, nor swallow a piece of another human. I bring this story up to illustrate a little of what I've learned from silence. You may say that all these things are not enough, but they are good things—though my methods of study were unorthodox.

By proposing a college student who bites people as a model of humanity, I will certainly anger some. But I have my reasons. A violent-tempered person given to using his teeth is yet unwilling to swallow the flesh of others: there's something particularly powerful about this lesson. Besides, during the course of the Cultural Revolution we scarcely had any better models to learn from.

---

33. Brownian motion is the random movement of a particle as a result of collision with surrounding liquids or gaseous molecules. It is named after the botanist Robert Brown, who discovered the phenomenon in 1827.

For a time you would often hear older people saying our generation was no good; among us were the Red Guards of the Cultural Revolution who were of low character. Considering that we weren't products of orphanages but brought up properly in schools, our families and teachers ought to bear a certain responsibility for our poor behavior. And really, everyone concerned themselves altogether too much with our moral conduct. Later, we were sent to work in the countryside, and there we were very kind and considerate to one another. This, at least, is worth noting. My personal experience can serve as proof: once, during the harvest seasons, I got very sick and thought I was done for. No one came to care for me except for a classmate who was also sick, but who nevertheless half-carried, half-dragged me across the Namwan River to the hospital. Though the river wasn't deep, it was a good five kilometers wide at that time; it had flooded so you couldn't even find the riverbanks. Supposing someone else had become sick, I would have done the same for them. It's things like this that make me think we weren't bad at all, and there was no need to bury ourselves in the countryside and never return, nor to take certain hints and commit mass suicide, making space for the next generation. For all that was good about our character and our behavior, we must thank the teachings of silence.

4

There's one thing that the majority of people know: that we can choose between a culture of discourse and a culture of silence. I've experienced many such opportunities to choose. For example, in the countryside, some of my teammates chose to say a little something, and went to the "Activists' Congress" to "share their learning," expecting to derive some benefit from it. Some of our younger friends may be unfamiliar with these terms, which I'll explain briefly: An Activists' Congress was a Congress of Activists in the Living Study and Implementation of Chairman Mao's Works, and to share one's learnings was to talk about one's experiences and gains in the course of living out Chairman Mao's teachings. Anyone attending the congress was an activist, and to be an activist was a good thing. A further opportunity was—provided you spoke up during the congress and were active in social movements—to become a student cadre, and being a student cadre was also a good thing. I happily passed up both of these opportunities. Now, those who have chosen the culture of speech may not believe that I passed them up of my own accord. They may think I was simply not a good speaker or didn't make the grade, that I wasn't worthy of speech. Speech is power, and power is yet another good thing, and many people go to great lengths to enter the circles of discourse, even struggling over the "right to speak." If I say I willingly gave this up, some will not believe me—fortunately, there are also many who will. My main reason was that, once you've entered these circles, then you must speak their language, you must even use their language to think, and I find this tiresome. As I see it, those circles are mired in anemia.

Twenty years ago I was a sent-down youth[34] in Yunnan. How the local people viewed us, besides noting that we dressed a little better and had whiter skin, is a complete mystery to me. I believe they thought of us as people standing onstage, and felt they had to speak to us in theatrical language—at least, that's how they thought when we first arrived. This was a mistake, of course, but it was not offensive. A more offensive mistake was that they believed we were all rich and did everything they could to hike the marketplace prices, to the point where we were paying two or three times what the locals paid for every little thing we bought. Later, we learned an unusual trick for shopping: instead of bargaining, we'd

---

34. "Sent-down youth" refers to young people who, beginning in the 1950s and until the end of the Cultural Revolution (1976), were sent from urban to rural areas to work instead of receiving a scholastic education.

toss them a wad of mao bills and let them count it, meanwhile we'd walk off with whatever we wanted to buy. By the time they'd finished counting, both buyer and goods were gone. In the beginning we would give a fair price, but later, some of us gave less and less, even mixing fen in with the mao. Even if I were to proclaim myself innocent, that I'd never done this sort of thing, you'd never believe me, so I'll make no contentions. One day one of the students was finally grabbed by a villager while he was paying like this—of course, I don't mean myself. The villager had made up his mind to thrash the student, but he first stammered and stuttered and at last spat out: "Hey! No! Mao's Thought, eh? Resist Individualism!" Later, we went home and laughed ourselves into convulsions over what he'd said. These days, as you can imagine, the villager might say something like: "Hey! No! Four Emphases, eh? Five Beauties!" and we would laugh ourselves to death just the same. I give this example not to take cheap shots or to be clever, but to illustrate the impoverishment of speech. Using it to actually say anything becomes difficult, let alone using it to think.

I passed many years in silence: in the countryside, as a worker, as a college student, and later as a teacher at university. Keeping silent as a teacher sounds impossible, but I taught technical courses and only spoke technical language at the podium, and I vanished as soon as class was out. The way I see it, you can keep silent no matter what it is you do. Of course, I also had a lifelong passion for writing fiction, but I never tried to publish what I wrote, I still maintained my silence. The reasons for this silence are simple: I could not trust those who belonged to the circles of speech. The experiences of my short life had taught me that those circles were nothing but yammering madhouses. What I doubted then was not just the group that said a mu of land could produce three hundred thousand jin of grain and talked about a spiritual atomic bomb—I doubted all societies of speech. If you could prove to me today that

I'd mistakenly committed a grave generalization, my happy relief would know no bounds.

5

You may not believe me when I say I kept silent for so many years; you weren't born yesterday, after all. You don't believe that I've never "stated my position" during a meeting; that I have never written a criticism, and you'd be right to doubt: I can prove neither that I am mute nor that I am illiterate, and in truth I have done both the stating and the criticizing. By my standards however, none of that is real speech, but instead the payment of a kind of speech tax. We've heard that, in years past, even great people sometimes "spoke contrary to their own hearts," and thus we can see that the tax is applied very broadly indeed. Because of the speech tax we cannot be held responsible for everything that we have said: our superiors made us say it. But if all speech is only a payment of tax, then we're in trouble. What can all that speech be used for? It's talk, not money. It can't be used to build dams, nor power stations. Once paid, it can only be left there to rot, to be mocked by future generations. Of course, I shouldn't concern myself about the uses of expropriated speech; perhaps it has other functions I've not thought of. What I want to say is, the collection of the speech tax has been going on since ancient times. Those who speak have always known of the need to pay it. That need has been absorbed into their blood, and realized in their mouths.

There's an example of this in the classic Chinese novel *The Story of the Stone*, in which two young girls are playing a game of poetic free-association in the garden. Line follows after line, and eventually out comes something from the ancient *Book of Songs*.[35]

---

35. *The Book of Songs* is the oldest of the Chinese classics, a collection of 305 songs dating back over two thousand years to the Zhou dynasty. They are considered the basis of Confucianism and later of Chinese literature.

It was discouraging to read: a couple of teenage girls, in their own backyard in the middle of the night, and still they feel obliged to quote *The Book of Songs*. Unpacking this a little more carefully, of course, it's the author who has the real problem: the unshakeable compulsion, when speaking, to pay the speech tax. I believe that the world of speech varies between two extremes. At one extreme is the speech of sages, which is freely given. At the other is the speech of the silent, which is coin levied by force. All speech between these two extremes is difficult to resolve: it is both an offering, and an appropriation. There is a tax official in the hearts of all those who speak. Chinese scholars have a very strong sense of their obligation to society, but this is only speech taxation, it is being a good taxpayer. That may be an ugly way of putting it; a better way would be to say they take the troubles of the world upon their shoulders.

I once was a silent person, meaning that I did not like to speak in meetings, nor to write articles. Recently, this much has changed: I'll speak during meetings, and occasionally write a little something. I have had a strong reaction to this change, and feel as though I lost my childhood innocence. It means betraying years of long-standing practice; that I no longer belong to the silent majority. This not only causes me pain, but also a faint sense of depression. The resumption of speech does not mean the resumption of my tax-paying responsibilities—if that were the case, I would be nothing but a giant basket of nonsense. My responsibilities lie elsewhere.

A few years ago, I participated in some sociological research and thus came into contact with some marginalized groups, the most unusual of these being homosexuals. After doing this research, I suddenly realized: the so-called minority groups were simply groups whose speech went unsaid. Because they had not spoken out, other people thought they didn't exist, or were very distant. People still don't believe that homosexuals exist in China. Abroad, people know homosexuals exist, but don't know who they are. Two scholars in the humanities wrote a book entitled *Word is Out*. Later, I had another sudden understanding: that I belonged to the greatest disadvantaged group in history, the silent majority. These people keep silent for any number of reasons, some because they lack the ability or the opportunity to speak, others because they are hiding something, and still others because they feel, for whatever reason, a certain distaste for the world of speech. I am one of these last groups and, as one of them, I have a duty to speak of what I have seen and heard.

6

Most of what I write falls into the category of literature. In my opinion, so-called literature should go like this: just write well, and to hell with the rest of it. I can think of nowhere but literature where my odd ideas would fit in. Blame literature for giving me a foothold within this circle; a foothold from which I can attack the circle itself, and attack the entire world of the yang.

A few years ago, I was studying in America. Someone there once asked me: You Chinese people talk about yin and yang; how come all good things belong to the yang, and nothing good is left for the yin? This is because the right to speak belongs to the yang, so, of course, it will have nothing good to say about the yin. Confucius himself couldn't avoid this convention, and attacked "women and people of mean character" as a lump. This phrase of his has been repeated for thousands of years, but I have never heard a single response from the subjects of the attack. Everyone takes pains not to be seen as a person of mean character, but no one has yet resolved the question of how not to be a woman. Even in this modern age, female-to-male sex change operations are a point of contention. Put simply, the things that are said in the circles of speech will never meet with rebuttal. You could be charitable and call this "saying one's piece"; it could be described less charitably with a popular phrase describing immoral behavior: "Beating the deaf, cursing the mute, and trampling on graves." But I know one fact for absolute certain: anyone who speaks will do so imperfectly, even saints will speak imperfectly, and these imperfections are not trivial.

By now I have also wormed my way into the circles of speech, and this can only mean one thing: those circles are already crumbling. In light of this unfortunate truth, there have been many calls to action: We must shore up China's spiritual structure, and so forth. As someone originally from a different circle, I have a suggestion for my friends in this new one: Let us examine ourselves. Have we become stupid? Have we become mad? There are many mirrors that can be used for self-examination: Chinese tradition is one, foreign culture is another. Another, even larger mirror is right by our side—the silent majority. All this is simply spoken from the heart, of course. A few years ago, when I had just emerged from silence, I wrote a book and gave it to someone I respected. He didn't like the book, he thought that books weren't supposed to be like that. In his view, books should educate the people, and elevate their souls—and these words are worth their weight in gold. But among all the people of the world, the one I wish most to elevate is myself. This is contemptible; it is selfish; it is also true.

ESSAYS

George Orwell

'Political writing in our time consists almost entirely of prefabricated phrases bolted together like the pieces of a child's Meccano set. It is the unavoidable result of self-censorship. To write in plain, vigorous language one has to think fearlessly, and if one thinks fearlessly one cannot be politically orthodox'

These essays, reviews and articles illuminate the life and work of one of the most individual writers of this century – a man who created a unique literary manner from the process of thinking aloud and who elevated political writing to an art

'Anyone who wants to understand the twentieth century will still have to read Orwell' Timothy Garton Ash, *New York Review of Books*

HALF A LIFELONG ROMANCE

Eileen Chang

'They were, he felt, like children who had made a terrible mistake'

When shy young engineer Shijun meets factory worker Manzhen, he is captivated by her hopeful nature and gentle beauty, and a relationship between them quickly blossoms. But family pressures and events beyond their power soon destroy the possibility of their future together. Can the pair find their way back to each other? Or will the trauma of their past obscure the way? Set in 1930s Shanghai, *Half a Lifelong Romance* is a rich and moving tale of love, hopefulness and the malign forces that – despite our greatest efforts – can overwhelm us.

'A dazzling and distinctive writer' *The New York Times Book Review*

UNDER THE SIGN OF SATURN

Susan Sontag

Susan Sontag's third essay collection brings together her most important critical writing from 1972 to 1980. In these provocative and hugely influential works she explores some of the most controversial artists and thinkers of our time, including her now-famous polemic against Hitler's favourite film-maker, Leni Riefenstahl, and the cult of fascist art, as well as a dazzling analysis of Hans-Jürgen Syberberg's *Hitler: a Film from Germany*. There are also highly personal and powerful explorations of death, art, language, history, the imagination and writing itself.

'After this feast, I am eager for her thoughts on anything' *Chicago Sun Times*

THE FIRE NEXT TIME

James Baldwin

James Baldwin's impassioned plea to 'end the racial nightmare' in America was a bestseller when it appeared in 1963, galvanizing a nation and giving voice to the emerging civil rights movement. Told in the form of two intensely personal 'letters', *The Fire Next Time* is at once a powerful evocation of Baldwin's early life in Harlem and an excoriating condemnation of the terrible legacy of racial injustice.

'The great poet-prophet of the civil rights movement ... his seminal work' *Guardian*

THE ORIGINS OF TOTALITARIANISM

Hannah Arendt

Hannah Arendt's chilling analysis of the conditions that led to the Nazi and Soviet totalitarian regimes is a warning from history about the fragility of freedom, exploring how propaganda, scapegoats, terror and political isolation all aided the slide towards total domination.

'Perhaps Arendt's most profound legacy is in establishing that one has to consider oneself political as part of the human condition. What are your political acts, and what politics do they serve?' *Guardian*